STUDY AND SUCCEED

WITHDRAWN

F-

STUDY

AND

JOHN WILEY AND SONS, INC.

NEW YORK · LONDON

SUCCEED

LYLE TUSSING

DEPARTMENT OF PSYCHOLOGY

EL CAMINO COLLEGE

Library of Congress Catalog Card Number: 62-8792
Printed in the United States of America

PREFACE

This book was written for the student who wants to use his energy effectively in doing his school work and the student who wants to improve his study techniques. It is also designed to give help in developing an understanding of the college environment.

Many instructors have observed that the average student who studies in the library has a certain behavior pattern. To begin with, he usually has trouble finding time to get to the library. Once there, he faces the problems of finding a good seat, looking up his assignment, and getting down to work, while looking around for acquaintances.

When this student finally starts to work, it is with an attitude of "Why must I go through this torture?" As he reads through the assignment, he keeps a finger at the end as a timing device, something like a three-minute egg indicator. By holding up the part read and the part to be read so he can compare their thicknesses, the "egg" is labeled "hard" or "soft."

This example illustrates the point that college students are constantly told they must study hard to succeed, but seldom are they actually given instruction in how to study. In our rapidly changing world, there is so much knowledge available that it is necessary to learn rapidly in order to keep up with the increasing amount of data. This book discusses a number of methods the student can use to help increase his learning efficiency and utilize the information he acquires to the best advantage.

Many students have particular study problems that must be overcome. For instance, there are those who follow the lines in the book with their index fingers as they read. One almost gets the impression that they hope someone will ask if they have covered the assignment, because they can honestly say they have covered every word (with their fingers).

Some students use the "ethereal" or "off-in-space" study technique. While the eyes act like a radar, scanning the required space to be read (but recording nothing), the mind is manufacturing many fascinating ideas on "cloud nine."

Through the use of sound psychological principles, we have tried to find solutions for these and other problems faced by college students in making their adjustment to college life. It is hoped this will aid in their transition from "busy" students to efficient scholars.

LYLE TUSSING

Green Valley Lake, California
November, 1961

See as Much as you can

Learn from WHAT you See

Read WITH an intent to Learn

Study WHERE you can Read

Understand HOW to Study

Know WHEN *you* Understand

(Read the above from top to bottom, then from bottom to top.)

ACKNOWLEDGMENTS

I wish to acknowledge the many suggestions and aids that were given by a number of instructors and deans of men and women; their names are not given because of the lack of space, but their contributions are appreciated.

There is, however, special thanks to be given to Mr. Charles Schlerf, who has illustrated many of the ideas in this book so appropriately. Also, I wish to express my appreciation of the tremendous amount of work done by Mrs. Miriam Kadison in research, editing, and assembling the material into its final form. In addition, thanks are due to John Wiley and Sons for their permission to reproduce some of the pages and ideas from *Psychology for Better Living*.

L. T.

CONTENTS

1
THE COLLEGE ENVIRONMENT

THE COLLEGE ATMOSPHERE

The atmosphere of college may at first seem rather indifferent because of an apparent lack of concern for you as an individual. However, the facilities for developing yourself are available if you will but put forth the effort. The college is set up for mature people; you must act like an adult in using your independence to find the best way to fit yourself into the adult world.

The College Catalogue

The most important feature of a college is the educational material that is available to you through the courses offered. The appearance of the campus and the organization of social activities are not important in attaining your educational goals. A large amount of information that is often overlooked by the student is very carefully summarized in the college catalogue. Each year, colleges publish these bulletins which contain the latest information about courses, registration, counselling services, credits, and requirements for fulfilling a major or minor in a specific subject field and for graduation.

There is additional information about library facilities, grade points, scholarships, financial assistance,—in fact, all activities connected with the school's educational program. It is well worth your time to go over the book minutely, page by page, and make sure that your selection of courses will help you toward your goal in the college you have selected. After you have studied your

1

catalogue you will have a greater knowledge of the steps to take in pursuing your educational program.

Deciding on a College Program

The entering college student must be realistic in his choice of courses. He must evaluate his learning skills and

determine his vocational or professional goals before deciding on this college program.

It might be helpful to know some of the qualities and abilities which many companies who hire college graduates consider very important. A survey [1] reported by the Department of Labor revealed a number of shortcomings (see list) which 182 companies found among recently employed college people. The starred items are discussed in succeeding chapters on the pages indicated.

Required Courses

In our great desire to become educated individuals it is necessary for us to have points of common knowledge and be able to communicate together. Courses have been developed to produce this broader base and, in most colleges, are included in what might be considered a basic curriculum. These courses have been tested through a great number of years and the lead-

SHORTCOMINGS AS INDICATED BY THE COMPANIES	NUMBER OF COMPANIES REPORTING
Overemphasis on management positions; expect too much too soon	68
Unrealistic idea of what is expected in business	48
°Lack of ability to write clearly and concisely (pages 40–42, 91–97)	46
°Inability to speak effectively (pages 40, 42, 91–99)	45
°Lack of specific goals; failure to determine what they want to do (pages 142–154)	23
°Failure to recognize the value of experience and on-the-job training (pages 35, 142–154)	19
°Immaturity; poor social judgment (pages 141–144)	16
°Unrealistic appraisal of their own abilities (pages 145–148)	12
Overemphasis on salary and benefits	7
°Lack of motivation and drive (pages 24–25)	6

ers in business and industry, as well as the instructors in college, agree that with this broad background a person is going to be much more able to handle himself in an effective manner in our persent busy world. Quite often the college student is needlessly concerned over the amount of time that these courses will take away from what he considers his "real" educational goal. He wants to delve into the specifics immediately. However, it must be remembered that each required course may act as a foundation for something even more specific. For example: an interest in life sciences can lead from a broad study of zoology, to entomology, down to concentration on the numerous species of aphides. There is no end to the specifics that man is investigating at the present time, but to be considered well-educated, a person must have a general overview of man's accumulation of knowledge in a great many fields.

In many large companies today, personnel managers are interested in prospective employees' background of general knowledge. After the employee is hired he is trained in handling specific jobs according to company policy.

The successful salesman who holds the top positions not only knows the product he sells, but draws from knowledge he has accumulated in many diverse fields which may be of prime interest to his prospective customer.

An engineer must be extremely proficient in mathematics and science, but he should also be aware of basic knowledge in what might appear to be remotely unrelated areas. Without this awareness of other subjects he

might be considered an outstanding engineer, but not necessarily a culturally informed person.

Nevertheless, one of the big problems facing many students is developing interest in required courses. A mental block seems to develop toward these courses because students resist having to take them without any choice in the matter. We all like to feel that we are mature and are able to make good judgments; we believe that we know better than anyone what is going to be good for us in the life situations we foresee. Since our judgment is threatened, we may want to oppose the force that dictates we must learn this material and prove to the world that we do not have to learn it. This does not resolve the problem nor does it help us to get through the situation with the least amount of effort.

How are we to develop interest in subjects that others feel would be good for us? First of all, we must accept the fact that it is quite possible to learn something from these courses that will give us a fuller understanding of the world. Also, we should realize that our tastes are acquired; we probably did not like solid food when it was first presented to us, or perhaps we did not like olives. Many of the conditions in our environment may at one time have been somewhat distasteful. But the foods which were once disliked may have become delicacies, and unwelcome situations may have become sought after, enjoyable experiences after we have tried them and become familiar with them. Recognize that the best way to enjoy any experience or any situation in life is to approach it with a zest for the new and the unusual.

Another factor is involved in the dislike of certain required courses. We have all known girls who shy away from chemistry or mathematics and boys who do not care to study English and languages. The reason for this is that the members of each sex have certain areas in which they can succeed and other areas in which they do not feel adequate or produce as well as the opposite sex. Since no one wants to compete and fail, there is a desire to avoid those activities which may end in failure.

However, if we bypass those areas more easily mastered by the opposite sex, we will not be able to communicate well. We live in a world in which we must try to have some understanding of the principles involved in all of man's activities. By striving for this understanding, we become better marriage partners; we will be more willing to accept the proficiencies of the opposite sex and to be sincerely humble about our own learning limitations.

If a student is unable to see the practical value of a course, he is fighting a losing battle. Before enrolling in such a course, it might be wise to investigate the ways in which the material to be learned might be used in life situations. A talk with the instructor who is going to teach the course would probably be very beneficial, since he has felt the subject is worthwhile and has devoted a considerable time to making it a good share of his life's enjoyment. Perhaps some of this enthusiasm and feeling of worth for the course may rub off on the student as he probes and questions the usefulness of spending time and effort to learn the material.

Instructors

Instructors are not substitutes for mother and father; they are people who are there to impart information that you may want to obtain. They are not going to spoon-feed you, but they will encourage honest effort on your part and will be glad to help you if you are having trouble. Most instructors recognize the apple-polishing technique and shy away from being substitute parents. Don't overlook the obvious way to put yourself in the instructor's good graces, which is coming to class wide awake and being interested in what he has to say.

Classroom Behavior

Develop good classroom manners by following these rules:

1. Be on time, and explain any particular reason for lateness or absence.

2. Avoid cutting classes. Besides missing important lecture material, you may annoy the teacher, and your grade may be affected.

3. Participate in class discussion and help to keep it alive. Don't depend on others to do all the volunteering.

4. Don't prepare to leave class before the period is over. It is rude to the teacher and distracting to the class.

Although teachers have office hours for student conferences, it often saves time to ask short questions after class, immediately after the subject has been discussed. This permits the instructor to clarify a point for the student without taking time from his office hour. Be sure to keep all appointments you make with teachers, since they are usually very busy.

HELPING YOURSELF BECOME A BETTER STUDENT

If you will follow the suggestions in this book, you will notice improvement in your ability to study and learn. It takes time and patient effort to change any habit, and this is particularly true of improving study habits. Determination for self-improvement of any kind leads to a happier life. If you will remain firm in your desire to learn more efficiently, you will be rewarded not only with better grades but a better adjustment to life.

Following is a list of ten common study problems that students face. Check those that bother you most. You will find each discussed on the page indicated.

Reference

1. Frank S. Endicott, "Employment of College Graduates in Business and Industry, 1960," *Occupational Outlook Quarterly*, U. S. Department of Labor, Bureau of Labor Statistics, IV:2:24–28.

Ten Common Study Problems Students Face

Check those that bother you most.   You will find each discussed on the page indicated.

1. (   ) Unable to find a motive for study; lack of interest in course (pages 29–39)

2. (   ) Procrastination; cannot start studying immediately (pages 30–31)

3. (   ) Cannot select important points in an assignment (pages 36–38)

4. (   ) Cannot concentrate; daydreaming (pages 14, 19)

5. (   ) Cannot make useful notes (pages 80–89)

6. (   ) Slow reader (pages 54–71)

7. (   ) Cannot study because of interruptions by other persons (pages 16–19)

8. (   ) Outside work too heavy to allow enough time for study (page 21)

9. (   ) Social activities interfering with study time (pages 19–28)

10. (   ) Cannot allot adequate time for courses; neglect of and disinterest in some courses (pages 19–28)

2
LEARNING AND STUDY

THE NEED FOR
AN EDUCATIONAL GOAL

The best way to study still remains a mystery for many students even in this scientific age. Students who have high intellectual ability may not be fulfilling their capacities and expectations because they have not learned the correct way of assembling material and utilizing their time effectively. Some students say they just don't know how to "get with it."

It is important to settle down and study with a real purpose. To take classes aimlessly deprives one of the satisfaction of knowing that the best use of his energy has been made. The setting of an educational goal requires purposeful direction of activity. It will often be a means of compelling one to take action.

There are two kinds of goals. The first is an immediate goal which must be achievable and must exert some pressure on the student to make him want to find a solution and relieve the pressure. The second, the remote goal, should be one that has potential for improving his status, his feeling of worth in his family and community, or his desire to make something of himself. The remote goal can also exert pressure, but it is slow and gradual and does not bring about an immediate release of tension.

The study period should be looked on as training for the activities that will take place later in life. A person who has good habits and well-developed skills in tackling the problem of study will probably be able to utilize them to become successful at a later date.

WHAT IS LEARNING?

The basic principles that psychologists generally accept as related to learning are: [1]

1. Native intelligence or ability are, in part, determiners of what can be taught and how it can be best retained.

2. People learn best when they are psychologically and physiologically ready to assimilate the subject matter. Many of our motor skills, such as hand-eye coordination, can be learned only when there has been adequate physiological development. In activities such as reading, the eye muscles must be developed to see small letters and differences (p, d, q, b). In writing, muscles must be developed and controlled to make small integrated movements rather than large gross movements.

3. Learning comes through repetition and drill, which, when used on some materials, seem to make them more accessible and more readily acquired. However, it is not just a matter of continually going over the material, but of having the material make an additional impression on the organism.

4. Learning seems to take place best when there are satisfactory results. When there is pleasure, enjoyment, and happiness resulting from the learning, improvement comes more rapidly and the learning time is shortened.

5. Best results are obtained when the material to be learned has meaning or the activity "makes sense." The more meaningful the material, the more a person can see that it is useful and can put it into operation in daily living, the easier it will be for the person to remember and the longer the material will be retained.

6. There is also an indication that many people learn when they understand the relationship of the part to the whole, or the relationship of the whole to the parts Teaching by making a pattern with the integration of units is more readily understood by the student than just non-related material. The interrelating of one part to the other makes for an easy comprehension in the learning process.

One or all of these principles is utilized by the skillful teacher. He will motivate by having the student understand relationships, use discipline in memorization, and develop the desire and excitement of curiosity in conquering the new and unexplored areas. Not long ago, the Educational Policies Commission in its book, *Education for All American Children,*[2] explained the teaching and learning process in this manner:

1. Growth and development are continuous.
2. Behavior is learned.
3. Learning and growth are stimulated by both security and adventure.
4. Each individual is unique.
5. We learn what we live.
6. We always learn several different things at the same time.
7. We learn a great deal, and learn it durably, by example.

These ideas have been stated in many educational psychology books in different ways. Nevertheless, these concepts are building blocks that can be utilized in obtaining a better understanding of the learning process. The more we can develop and utilize these processes, the easier it will be for us to get an education.

Learning is evidenced by a change in our behavior. If there were no changes, we would not learn. This aids us in aiming our behavior toward perfection. However, this same change creates inconsistencies which may block our path and lead us away from the perfection we seek. The solution to this problem cannot lie in any mysterious process. It is the direct outcome of the efforts of human beings to use their resources, their bodily equipment, their experiences, and their training to make adjustments that are necessary to solve the problem.

In order to keep pace with today's changing world we need more knowledge than ever before. Without the process of learning, we could not profit from past experiences; with learning, we move toward greater control and domination of our environment and the subsequent rewards.

Learning may be regarded as a *progressive organization of behavior.* In its simplest form, it involves a response to an already present stimulus for new behavior. Learning is partly the discovery of what we do in a given situation and partly a matter of separating the significant factors from the insignificant ones in order to react adequately to them. From the developmental point of view, learning is the recognition and mastery of the successive number of life situations one has to face.

Much of an individual's success in life depends upon the ease and confidence with which he acquires knowledge and

STUDY HABITS INVENTORY

This list of statements concerns study habits and general scholastic attitudes. After each statement, place an X in the particular column which expresses your behavior. This list is discussed in the last part of the chapter and a key is provided for scoring your responses.

	Yes — Generally this is true	Undecided — Sometimes this happens	No — Never or rarely
1. When I read or study I have a tendency to pick out unimportant points instead of important ones.		✓	
2. It is difficult for me to concentrate on reading assignments because I'm not interested in my school work.		✓	
3. I have trouble understanding what I read.	✓		
4. I like to read and wish I had more time to devote to reading.	✓		
5. I often find I am too sleepy or tired to study.	✓		
6. I keep a dictionary near me when I study, and I use it.	✓		
7. I have a definite place in which to do my studying.	✓		
8. I don't have an organized plan of studying.	✓		
9. When I study, I set a goal for the amount of material I want to cover.	✓		
10. My studies suffer because of the time I waste reading the newspaper, watching television, etc.		✓	
11. During a lecture, I copy notes on earlier material and miss important points being made by the teacher.		✓	
12. I cut classes whenever there is something more interesting to do or when I have to cram for a test.		✓	
13. I try hard to make a good grade, even though I may not like a course.	✓		
14. When I memorize material, I learn only what is absolutely necessary.	✓		
15. I read over my lecture notes as soon after class as possible.			✓
16. I forget what I learn in class.		✓	
17. I say and do things without thinking.			✓
18. When I read an assignment, I write down the main points to help me remember.			✓
19. I could do better in school if I didn't dislike some of my courses and teachers.	✓		
20. I worry about being lazy.	✓		
21. I work on my assignments regularly and keep them up to date.		✓	

STUDY HABITS INVENTORY (*Continued*)

	Yes	Undecided	No
	Generally this is true	Some-times this happens	Never or rarely
22. Because I find it difficult to express myself in writing I am slow in turning in written assignments.			✓
23. I am too careless.			✓
24. In studying for a test I arrange facts in logical sequence—by date, order of importance, etc.	✓		
25. I get so nervous during exams that I can't concentrate and tell all I know.	✓		
26. Before I start to answer essay-type exam questions, I plan the answer in my mind.		✓	
27. I can't finish tests within the time allowed, although I work the entire period.		✓	
28. When I check returned tests or written work, I find that careless errors lowered my grade.	✓		
29. I dislike a particular teacher and neglect the work for his class.			✓
30. The main reason I'm going to school is the prestige of having a college education.			✓

upon his ability to perform tasks and activities that occur in life situations. One humorist said that education gives you a lot of things to worry about which the ignorant ignore completely. Actually, the more knowledge we have at hand, the greater our capacity for enjoying our environment.

How We Learn

Some individuals think there is a magic mental button to be pushed which will disclose short cuts to learning. *There is no magic button.* Learning takes place because a person,

through the central nervous system, is exposed to material which the organism feels is important in maintaining security or in obtaining mental and physical well-being.

The learner knows his world through the use of his senses. The response he makes will utilize both his past and present experiences together with his recognition of present activity. All of these are part of the total process known as *perception*.

We are continually bombarded with stimuli from a great many areas, and obviously we do not respond to all the stimuli that reach the central nervous system. When we are very young we learn those responses which are going to protect us, help us develop a sense of security, and give us a sense of pleasure. Thus, we learn when to cry and when not to cry. We learn when to kick our feet and when to be quiet. We learn to interpret certain sounds, such as those of the parents who are going to feed us or make us more comfortable, or those of the barking dog or the telephone.

It may be seen that methods of learning are actually ways of recognizing and interpreting environmental situations to bring about comfort and proper reactions to environmental situations. Our adult methods of making ourselves comfortable in our environment may seem entirely different from the early, rudimentary actions of babyhood. We may study philosophy or history or political science in order to gain or maintain status. What we are actually maintaining is our concept of self. When we are threatened by the questions or problems dealing with specific information accumulated in the past, we feel adequate and competent in handling these problems. At times we feel somewhat superior because we have had training and can produce answers.

In our examination of the learning process we must not overlook the basic physical aspects of learning. The rate at which the individual will learn is dependent upon such physical qualities as the efficiency of the visual or the auditory system or the sensitivity of the nervous system to stimuli. Since an integration process must take place between the stimulus from the outside and the reaction of the person to the material presented, any deviation in the organism's physical capacity will have some effect upon the outcome. If the person is not able to respond because of an inadequate sensory system (receiving apparatus), or if, after the material is received, it does not seem to leave an impression on the central nervous system, then the amount of time or effort it takes to learn may be longer.

Association and learning. We learn by making associations. All the things we know at the present time are stored in our memory centers. If we are to learn a new concept, it is necessary to hook the new idea to those already known. The known ideas may be thought of as being on plaques with holes at the bottom, and the new ideas we wish to retain would have hooks on them. When we hook the new material onto the old material, it will be held securely. To say the same thing psychologically, the more bonds or fixations we can make between old and new ideas, the longer we will be able to remember the new and the easier it will be to recall. Build as many bonds and associations as possible between what is to be learned and what you already know.

Learning may also be classified into two types: (1) incidental, which occurs with little or no effort and has only a slight relationship to other things; (2) intentional, which is motivated through need and accomplished through effort (this type of learning may or may not be related to information previously learned).

There are times when it takes a great deal of effort to learn something. This may be due to the necessity of making new associations and establishing specific points of reference upon which additional material can be learned. Making intermediate associations will slow down the learner and subject matter will seem difficult. It must be realized that the development of this mental scaffolding helps to build the solid finished structure. However, it may require considerable time to bring together those basic principles necessary to solve a problem.

SUCCESSFUL LEARNING

Not all people who are outstanding have been good learners from the start. But anyone who wants to be outstanding must establish himself as a good learner. This type of person treats his problems as challenges, and learning situations the same way.

The poor learner may feel that success or failure is built into his physical being. Although having ability or lacking it may be influenced by physical or mental limitations to a degree, success is dependent upon the earnest

desire to satisfy one's curiosity. Education—or the accumulation of factual material—then becomes a process of organizing facts so that they can be utilized efficiently. Basically, the activity we call "study" is a receiving, storing, and shipping process.

Once we recognize what has to be done, it is necessary to determine the easiest way of stimulating the receptors that will take in the information for storage; the problem then becomes a matter of finding how the information, once it is taken in, can be recalled with greatest facility. This problem may be partly solved if we try to understand the general storage system involved in the process of learning.

In the storage of physical objects, it is practical to use square or rectangular boxes that fit together and then to stack these boxes in groups. Often they are placed on wooden skids so that a whole group may be moved at once. This process may be compared to developing a communality of words that may be expressed as ideas. Ideas may then be fitted together to form concepts. When we read new material, we are trying to store it into a mental warehouse for use at a future time when it can be used alone or with other ideas.

As we inspect accessible mental storage spaces, we also look at some of the interesting things already there. If we spend our time examining these stored ideas rather than storing the new material, we will not accomplish what we set out to do.

In many businesses, the items to be stored are numbered, catalogued, and filed for ready reference. This is probably the process the organism is going through in the storage of a new idea. The idea must be catalogued and placed with other ideas of a similar nature. This requires the examining of related subject areas. If this inspection of the material already stored is more interesting *than the filing* of the new, the activity of filing and making associations is slowed down and may even be disrupted. In other words, the mind will wander and concentration is made very difficult.

Improving Concentration

Concentrating on schoolwork is one of the biggest problems students have. They want to know how they can read an assignment without their minds wandering onto unrelated thoughts. As we have just seen, concentration is a matter of effectively storing information for ready reference. It requires real effort to ignore distracting thoughts. Successful learning is arrived at by improving concentration, a process that consists of:

1. Thinking only about what you want to think.
2. Holding your mind to the subject.
3. Excluding everything irrelevant to that subject.

These three objectives can be accomplished by:

1. Developing a deep interest.
2. Eliminating doubts about the subject.
3. Working rapidly and intensely.
4. Eliminating physical and emotional distractions.
5. Obtaining successful experiences which will beget greater concentration.

Motivation and Successful Learning

The process of getting a person into action may be referred to as motivating him. The teacher can motivate the student either by threatening him with punishment if he does not do the assigned task or by making the material interesting enough so the student will gravitate toward finding solutions to problems. Of course, in either instance, the receptiveness of the student to the stimulus is very important; the type of activity that may motivate one student may not be nearly so intriguing to another.

There are a number of factors that motivate us to learn. First of all, we learn because knowing the right way, the right pattern, or the best method of protection brings us greater security. This security, either mental or physical, brings a relief of tension which is highly pleasant.

Second, we learn because we want to communicate more adequately with our associates. This reason, as well as the others that follow, are actually a means of producing a satisfactory feeling of status and adjustment.

Third, we learn in order to bring the various phases of our environment into clearer focus; a greater understanding of our environment enables us to act more appropriately. In other words, we are able to act with less fear of threat because of a better perception of the details in the environment.

Fourth, we learn because we are continually making judgments, and we want to have adequate information so we can make good judgments. This may have the side effect of impressing others which in turn makes us feel good because we are respected. Also, making good judgments will help us to lead more pleasant, better-adjusted lives.

To sum up, we might say that effective learning takes place because of two basic motivations: the desire to obtain a thorough understanding of the environment, and the desire to be able to make judgments which bring about the feeling of personal worth to ourselves and others.

Deflection of motivation. When facts are presented to a person in a manner which enables him to identify himself with the outcome, a greater motivation is developed. However, if the task is drudging or hard to learn or offers no

challenge, motivation is weak or lacking. If, in addition, there is discouragement, punishment, sarcasm, or scolding in a person's environment, his learning can be slowed down to practically a stop.

There are many causes for motivation being less intense than desired. Most students wonder why they are not more interested in their school work. All work, including school tasks, requires some effort. A person will put forth the necessary effort only if he can obtain beneficial results. Also, work will be put off if the reward for the effort is either too remote or too small, or if the task is too unpleasant. Another reason for avoiding work is anticipation of failure and fear of the outcome.

We generally consider taking part in a baseball game as play, but to a man in the big leagues it is work. What makes the difference? At first glance it may appear that any endeavor in which a person can earn money may be thought of as work. But this is probably not the most important factor.

In general, work is a limiting activity of a person's behavior which follows

the wishes of others, but play is determined largely by one's own desires. A
student may find great pleasure in
reading a historical novel in his leisure
time, but reading the same novel as a
requirement for an English course may
be considered work and may be done
grudgingly.

The determining factor is not the
activity itself but the attitude of the
person toward it. If he can stop or
change his behavior at will, he is playing; if he has to follow the wishes and
dictates of someone else, he is working.

Laziness. There are students who
want to know why they are lazy in
school. They say, "I really don't want
to be lazy, but I just don't feel like
studying."

A student may be considered lazy
because it seems to others as if he
does not want to work. This may be
because the environment is not stimulating to him. However, he may not
be able to handle the problems in his
enviroment with feelings of enjoyment
and success.

All of us have heard this common
complaint made by parents: "The child
is lazy in school." What has actually
been said is that the school environment does not provide a need, and the
student does not gain satisfaction and
pleasantness from the tasks that are
presented. However, this same student may expend a tremendous amount
of energy in the football game after
school. This shows that he is receiving satisfaction from a different environment and task which can motivate
him to expend both mental and physical energy.

We can conclude from this that laziness does not necessarily have to be
considered as an over-all pattern of the
individual. It may be a very specific
reaction to a specific environment or
task.

The Desire to Learn

One of the most elusive and yet one
of the most important points in learning is the earnest desire to learn and
to remember. This seems so simple.
You may feel you would not be reading the material if you did not intend
to remember it. Too often, the task is
tackled with the idea that we have to
do it. Actually we may not be interested in learning the material at all.
However, it is possible to create a
greater capacity for wanting to learn
than many realize.

Some things are readily recalled if
you *really* want to know and express
yourself about a subject. A common
example of this is the material read in
the newspaper. A person does not
really study it but merely reads it
over once, and yet it leaves a lasting
impression. If you are interested in
finding out who is batting high in the
National League or the American
League, who is pitching for Cleveland,
or who was left on third base, you
look over the sports section casually,
probably reading it only once. The
next time you talk about these subjects,
the information is remembered easily.
You did not study the material, but you
have many facts at your fingertips.
Why? Because this is something you
really wanted to learn. It also follows
that if a student is *interested* in a school

subject it is much easier for him to comprehend and remember.

The continual drubbing in of facts will eventually leave impressions on the organism. However, unless there is an intent to learn, the drubbing-in method can result in parrot-like repetitions of cold little bricks of information that lack warmth and life. Without enjoyment or a satisfaction of curiosity, it is more difficult for assimilation of knowledge to take place. The desire to learn opens the doors to the receiving department and the information is ready for storage.

Learning in many ways is similar to eating. If the food is gulped and pushed in, it does not seem nearly as palatable and enjoyable as it is when eaten in quiet, peaceful surroundings where each mouthful can be thoroughly chewed and the taste appreciated. Under these favorable conditions, digestion and assimilation are more likely to proceed without discomfort, and one is less apt to have an upset or "nervous" stomach.

BLOCKS TO LEARNING

All factors affecting the process of interpretation become important factors in learning. The emotional set of the organism at a particular time has a great deal to do with how a situation will be evaluated and acted upon. For instance, if the situation produces fear and threat, it may be difficult to remember the details involved. An example of this is the person who is afraid of appearing ignorant; he will concentrate on ways to defend himself rather than on learning the material presented.

Some students have made this remark about an instructor: "I do not think I will ever be able to learn anything from this person." Immediately after they have mentally or verbally said these words, they have developed blocks for themselves. Anything this instructor tries to teach becomes more difficult for these people to learn. It may be much better for a student to select another instructor than continue in a situation in which he is blocking his source of information. Unknowingly, he may be prohibiting himself from hearing, seeing, or understanding the material presented by this instructor.

Hate and holding grudges may be deterrents to efficient learning and study. A young man dropped out of high school to spite his father, whom he hated violently, and went to work. He moved from one position to another; finally, he decided he would be greatly benefited by returning to school and learning blueprint-reading and drafting. However, the instructor reminded him of his father, and, needless to say, he was not able to pass the course. Even though he knew the right lines to draw and recognized the solution to the drafting problems, he would make mistakes. He became so intent on proving the instructor could not teach him anything that he was not able to absorb information about blueprint-reading and drafting. Who was hurt at the end of the course? Surely not the instructor.

There are other blocks that produce the same effect upon the learning process. The student who thinks, "I'm not going to be able to use this information," or, "Why spend my time learning this when I could be doing something useful or having fun?" will not be very successful in memorizing and retaining that subject matter.

Some people become so involved in thinking of their own wants and needs that they are not able to recognize the wants and needs of others. Consequently, their observation of life and problem situations is very narrow because they are not able to see or interpret the behavior of others. Their main concern is how others should treat *them*, how others should look after *them*, and the effect that others are going to have upon *them*. Therefore, learning material must be pre-

sented to them in a way which follows a specific form or else they will not be able to utilize it. A student may completely disregard all the remarks of an instructor who does not talk in outline or who makes some error in English or pronunciation. A general statement may be missed. A specific statement that does not apply in all phases to their behavior or learning will not be accepted.

There are students who are very rigid in their ideas and make very limited changes in their behavior. Any subject matter presented to them has to be exactly fitted into their thinking, and even then there is little likelihood they will want to make a change.

If material seems too remote, it may be difficult to remember. For example, many students have trouble with history. This may be due to their inability to see a direct relationship between past happenings and those activities in which they are participating at the present. If they do not understand this relationship as they are studying, it is difficult for them to remember. They

must be able to identify with the subject area.

There are other emotional situations that produce very strong blocks. Love is one of them. The person in love finds it difficult to concentrate on the material at hand. He is so emotionally involved with another person that all other things lose value. Many a student has started at the top of the page and has read word after word until he has reached the bottom, only to find that he did not remember one word of one sentence because he was concentrating on his love life.

SCHEDULING TIME WISELY

One of the most important things a college student must learn is how to use his time effectively. If all his time were spent in study he would become a social misfit. But he would be just as much a misfit if all his time were spent in recreation or in doing things which would bring him immediate pleasure. Our adjustment in life is tied in with those goals and aspirations we wish to meet. In other words, we

are trying to develop an ideal self, the kind of individual we would like to be, who behaves as we would like to behave, either in the future or in an ideal setting.

Since we live in a society with other individuals, we must take part in social activities so that we may gain their acceptance and receive satisfaction in return. However, there are times when we are not happy in trying to please other people and want to get away from them and please ourselves. This vacillation from wanting to be accepted by others, to wanting to reach the ideal of our self, to wanting to just sit and contemplate life can create a disturbing internal situation. The good student recognizes that this internal conflict exists, and he will allocate a good share of his time to becoming the ideal personality or working toward the future goal.

A time schedule is a pattern which enables a student to see how his time is being used. If not enough time is allowed for study, he will feel inferior because he will not understand his assignments and will be unable to compete with his classmates. But if he does not give enough time to recreation and concentrates mostly on the pursuit of his future goal, he will be living without enjoyment in a confining, limited atmosphere. Therefore, in order to achieve an integrated life, the student should make a blueprint of his time and the needs and obligations that must be fulfilled.

There are always more things to be done than time to do them. A written plan for using time helps to show the relative value of one's activities; this

SAMPLE TIME SCHEDULE

Hours	Sunday	Monday	Tuesday	Wednesday	Thursday	Friday	Saturday
7–7:30		Breakfast					
7:30–8		Go to school					Breakfast and
8–9		English Class	Study	English	Study	English	go to Work
9–10	Breakfast	Study	Psych. Class	Study	Psych.	Study	Work
10–11	Church	History Class	Study	History	Study	History	
11–12		Art	Phys. Ed.	Art	Phys. Ed.	Art	
12–1	Dinner	Lunch					
1–2	Free	Study	Science Lab	Study	Science Lab	Study	
2–3	Study	Science Lecture		Science Lecture			
3–4		Free					
4–5		Work on job	Study	Work	Study	Work	
5–6	Free		Free		Free	Free	Free
6–7		Free / Dinner		Free			
7–8		Study	Study	Study	Study	Free	
8–9							
9–10		Free / Study	Free / Study	Free / Study	Free / Study		
10–11							
11–12							
12–							

aids in deciding what one really wants to accomplish and the most beneficial way to arrange one's time.

A time schedule should not be a hard taskmaster. It should allow the student to enjoy pleasant activities without anxiety, because time has also been allowed for work. Therefore, during the time allocated for recreation, the student should enjoy himself fully and not think about the school work that needs to be done. All this is basically a part of establishing a pattern for enjoying oneself in college and becoming more adequate to face problems in the years that follow college. The importance of recreation to the student is emphasized in the Department of Labor report (see Chapter 1). The companies responding to the questionnaire were in general agreement on several points regarding colleges and universities. Almost unanimously they rated extracurricular activities important in contributing to the all-round development of the student, and felt that participating in such activities during college years should be encouraged.

Just as the student must allow time for work and play, so must he leave some time unscheduled. If every hour of the day is reserved for some activity, a feeling of being a "slave" to a schedule can result. Since a student's life can be hectic and unforeseen activities can arise, a schedule must be elastic enough to take care of emergencies.

A sample time schedule is included here to show you how you might fill one out for yourself. You may prefer setting up a different form from the ones provided here for your use. Your schedule may be less detailed or even more detailed than the sample one shown on the preceding page.

Arranging the Time Schedule

Work out your schedule for spending your time, using the suggestions and charts which follow. Then use your time chart as an improved (but flexible) guide for your activities.

1. Make a record of how your time is actually spent. (Use the blank schedule provided unless you prefer to make your own.) Study this record to see if you can make improvements. Are there any time-wasting activities that can be eliminated, allowing extra time for doing more important things? Which hours seem to be best for you to do the most effective studying? Do you have enough free time so that some activities can be shifted around if emergencies arise?

2. Make a new time chart; follow these steps first:

   a. Fill in hours for sleep, meals, toilet.

   b. Fill in all hours taken by both regular classes and laboratory periods.

   c. Fill in hours taken by work for which you are paid.

   d. Leave some unscheduled time for flexibility.

   e. Fill in hours given to any campus activities.

   f. Allot time for planned recreation.

3. Allow the major part of the remaining time to study periods, observing these principles:

   a. Allow enough time for each study period to prepare assignments completely.

   b. Do not allow long study periods

MY PRESENT WEEKLY SCHEDULE

Hours	Sunday	Monday	Tuesday	Wednesday	Thursday	Friday	Saturday
6-7							
7-8							
8-9							
9-10							
10-11							
11-12							
12-1							
1-2							
2-3							
3-4							
4-5							
5-6							
6-7							
7-8							
8-9							
9-10							
10-11							
11-12							
12-							

for assignments you enjoy but which can be done in a short time.

c. Longer study periods should be allotted for subjects which are new, involve much reading, or are difficult.

d. Try to plan 5-minute reviews between classes before the beginning of the next class.

e. Alternate subjects when making your study plan; changing the way of thinking required for different types of subjects is relaxing.

4. Remember these things when planning your study time:

a. Two short periods for one subject is usually better than one very long study period because it is easier to remain alert for shorter periods.

b. Distribute study sessions for each subject throughout the week rather than bunching them together.

MY REVISED WEEKLY SCHEDULE

Hours	Sunday	Monday	Tuesday	Wednesday	Thursday	Friday	Saturday
6–7							
7–8							
8–9							
9–10							
10–11							
11–12							
12–1							
1–2							
2–3							
3–4							
4–5							
5–6							
6–7							
7–8							
8–9							
9–10							
10–11							
11–12							
12–							

c. Retention of studied material is better if the study periods are located either 24 hours before or after class period.

d. Provide a definite amount of extra time for heavy weekly assignments, such as class reports, etc.

5. Try your time schedule out for a week; as you work with it, you will probably find ways to revise and improve it. Remember that your sched-

ule is not rigid and must be suited to *your* needs; it must never be thought of as inflexible so that you become a slave to it.

EVALUATING LEARNING SKILLS

Most college students probably feel that they understand themselves very well, but usually they do not know how to judge the efficiency of their learning skills. In order to be successful in school, each student must be able to determine what his learning strengths and weaknesses are. What are the qualities which a successful student possesses?

The early work of McKinney as well as of many other investigators in the field of study has indicated that being a good student is actually divided into many parts. Each one may be a deciding factor in the success or failure of one's efforts to handle himself well in the school environment.

The student must be able to read, concentrate, and memorize. He must have a good auditory and visual memory. However, instead of memorizing at random, he must recognize and remember those points which the instructor indicates as important.

Such learning skills as making judgments, forming generalizations, and solving problems must be developed by the student. Other important practical skills are organizing reading matter and making reading notes, making outlines from the material read, and developing good lecture notes.

A good student must also be able to compete with others by permitting

them to stimulate him, but at the same time must not become depressed when he is beaten or feels he has not been treated fairly.

One other skill that cannot be overlooked is the proper utilization of available time. The student must arrange a schedule that achieves a good balance between study and other activities.

These general abilities have been grouped into attitudes, techniques, and practices that have been proven to be characteristic of the good student:

STUDY INCENTIVES

He has a strong desire for success in college.

He tries to see the value of taking each course.

He tries to find good reasons for knowing the material in each course.

He selects a vocation and plans a tentative program.

He has some definite reasons for going to college.

CLASSROOM TECHNIQUES

He is active during most of the class time; if necessary, he forces himself to be active. He begins participating early in the course, because even a poor contribution is acceptable then.

He tries to understand the reasons for classroom procedures.

He asks questions in class if he does not understand something, asks after class, or goes to the teacher's office.

He reviews the classroom work shortly after the period is over while his notes are still fresh in his mind.

He prepares for class by thinking about the topic to be discussed previous to class time.

He maintains a critical and constructive attitude.

He attends class because he knows that it often takes much time to obtain the material that he has missed by being absent.

He prepares for an examination by doing the required work to the best of his ability.

He makes an effort to be calm during an examination.

He has a conference with his instructors if he is having trouble in any of his courses.

WORK PLANS

He has a schedule which specifies the time for each subject.

His study periods are neither too long nor too short.

He begins a study period with enthusiasm.

He rests when necessary and then returns to his studies.

He has a definite place which is used mainly for study and which suggests study when he is there.

His place of study does not have too much noise or too many disturbing people or distracting objects.

He allows time for recreation in his schedule.

STUDY TECHNIQUES

He gets an over-all view of the assignment and what he should know when he is finished studying; then he goes over the material carefully.

He stops at the end of each section of the assignment and reviews.

He makes some type of outline from which he can get the substance of the assignment.

He strives for accuracy.

He thinks about the meanings of the facts and the relationships between the facts and life.

He tries to overlearn when memorizing.

He uses spare occasions to review important points.

He avoids daydreaming.

He tries to associate any specific item that he must memorize to a related meaning.

He tests himself when he has finished studying in a way which is similar to class tests.

INFLUENCES ON EFFECTIVE STUDY

He tries to be in peak physical condition.

He has periodic physical examinations.

He checks his vision and hearing.

He cultivates good hygienic habits: regular hours for sleeping and eating, adequate nourishment, proper elimination, and sufficient outdoor exercise.

He attempts to overcome strong dislike of teachers and subjects by discussions with class colleagues.

THE STUDY HABITS INVENTORY

At the beginning of this chapter, you were asked to check your study habits and scholastic attitudes, using the Study Habits Inventory. The purpose of the Inventory is to help the student see some areas in which successful students differ from those who are not doing as well as they should. The student is able to see how his learning behavior compares with other students' patterns. Thus, a check list of this type may be helpful in improving your grades.

The author found that students often expressed a desire for a short check list that would enable them to estimate the effectiveness of their study habits and also to compare their scores with others. A preliminary inventory was made, using suggestions that other authors and counselors felt were good study procedures.

When this list was checked by a number of students, the results showed that some of the items were not good indicators of whether or not they were typical of good students or poor students. These were then eliminated, and the remaining items were given varying weights. The Study Habits Inventory now has some predictive value as to how "good" or "poor" students check the items.

The responses to certain items (such as number 15, concerning reading over lecture notes after class) were expected to show the typical behavior of "good" students. However, the results of a sample group showed that about the same percentage of good and poor students checked the "Yes" column. In fact, the poor students indicated that it was true of their behavior more often than the good ones did.

It may be that a poor student needs to review his notes after class in order to achieve better grades, but a good student may feel he does not have to. Perhaps this is true because of factors, such as degree of intelligence or time of study or methods used in studying, not fully explored in this study.* However, responses to some of the items— for example, numbers 21 (working on assignments regularly and keeping them up to date) and 24 (arranging facts in logical sequence when studying for a test)—do seem to indicate the expected pattern of behavior for the "good" student.

The Study Habits Inventory was tested on a sample of 250 women and 250 men students who were attending college for the first time. The chart shows their scores as related to their average high school grades.

High School Grades	Average Inventory Score
	Women
C− & D	−11
C	−8.9
A & B+	+8.4
	Men
C− & D	−7.6
C	−6.2
A & B+	+8.0

* The author realizes that more work needs to be done in evaluating the area of specific study habit techniques used by "good" and "poor" students. The Study Habits Inventory is merely a beginning.

In another sample of 150 students, both men and women, the scores ranged from −3.6 for those who made C's and D's in high school, to +5.6 for those who made A's and B's. There were some A and B students who made negative scores, but the majority had high positive scores. Those who did C and D work usually made negative scores.

At the end of the chapter, you will find a key giving the value for each statement in the Inventory; use this key to find your score. Some of the statements are weighted positively, others negatively. Be sure you are accurate in your scoring. Add up all the statements you have checked which have a positive (plus) value; then subtract the negative statements from this sum. You will probably find that if you make B or higher grades you will have a positive score; if you make C or D grades you may have a negative score. By using the statements to which you responded negatively as a guide, you may be able to change your study methods and improve your grades.

Check your study procedures against each item on the back cover. These suggestions have been found to produce more effective study habits as well as developing more efficient students.

References

1. Lyle Tussing, *Psychology for Better Living*, John Wiley and Sons, New York, 1959.

2. Educational Policies Commission, *Education for All American Children*, National Education Association of the U. S., Washington, D. C., 1948.

KEY TO STUDY HABITS INVENTORY

	Yes	Undecided	No
1.	−1	−1	+2
2.	−2	−1	+3
3.	−1	−1	+1
4.	+1	−3	+2
5.	−3	0	0
6.	+2	0	−2
7.	+1	−1	0
8.	−2	0	+1
9.	+1	0	−1
10.	0	−2	+2
11.	−3	−3	+3
12.	−1	−1	+1
13.	+3	−3	−3
14.	−2	+1	+3
15.	−1	+1	+2
16.	−4	0	+2
17.	−1	−2	+1
18.	+1	−1	0
19.	−2	+3	−2
20.	−2	0	0
21.	+2	−3	0
22.	−2	−2	+3
23.	−3	0	+2
24.	+2	−1	+1
25.	−3	0	+2
26.	+2	−1	−1
27.	−4	0	+2
28.	−2	+1	+2
29.	−2	−2	+1
30.	−3	0	0

Test Yourself on Chapter 2

1. What is perception? _____

   _____

2. Explain the two types of learning. _____

   _____

3. Name at least four of the basic principles psychologists believe to be related to learning. _____

   _____

4. Why is it important to set an educational goal? _____

   _____

   _____

5. Define an immediate goal; a remote goal. _____

   _____

6. How can emotions affect learning? _____

   _____

7. What factors can cause a weakening of motivation to learn? _____

   _____

   _____

8. Is laziness usually an over-all personality pattern? _____

   _____

   _____

9. How can a time schedule help a student become more successful socially? _____

   _____

   _____

10. What is meant by "identifying" with a subject area? _____

   _____

   _____

3

METHODS OF IMPROVING STUDY

CHANGING AND IMPROVING STUDY HABITS

Psychologically speaking, a habit is an automatic, learned behavior pattern that enables an individual to handle specific types of environmental situations easily. The student who has acquired good study habits has developed a behavior pattern which enables him to sit down and begin working on his assignments with a minimum of fuss and a maximum of concentration. Habit permits him to attend to routine matters connected with settling down to work without having to give them much thought.

Everyone going to school is faced with the problem of having to study from books and understanding what he hears in class. He should be able to utilize this knowledge when it is called for. The student needs to be realistic and efficient in study and classroom learning. How can he get the most from his education in school, and how can he use the information he acquires

to the best advantage? The first thing to do is evaluate the efficiency of his habits of study and decide where they need improvement.

The student with poor study habits must have a real desire to replace them with good ones or he will not be able to do so. After analyzing his study habits and definitely deciding which ones need improvement, there are a number of things a student can do.

1. Begin practicing the new habit immediately; it should not be put off until tomorrow or next Tuesday; as time goes on it will become harder and harder to start.

2. Do everything to avoid continuing the old habit. For instance, if he has been spending several hours a week talking with friends in the coffee shop but decides he needs to spend the time studying, he must not go to the coffee shop at that time, but go directly to his place of study. This is particularly important when the habit is just being formed.

3. In sitting down to a task which has to be done by a certain time (such as writing an outline for a term paper), the student should not wait until tomorrow in hopes of being "in a better mood." He needs to carry out the project at the time he has set for it or he may lose the drive and desire to do it.

4. Until the new habit becomes well-established, the student should not allow himself to backslide. If his new time schedule calls for studying a subject at 7:30 P.M., he should begin studying promptly at that time. If he is doing something else at 7:30, he should stop, go to his study place, and start to work at once. Although he may feel unable to concentrate, he will find that by going through the process involved in studying he will soon be actively engaged in learning.

Improvement of study habits may not go forward as fast as desired. The student must realize that he will make errors, but he should not give up.

Procrastination

Procrastination, although not generally thought of in this way, is actually a process of selecting activities which we hope will bring the most pleasure into our daily living. Many people put off doing one unpleasant job because they know that another one will follow which may also be unpleasant. For instance, dishwashing may be put off, and when it is begun the person may go through the dilly-dally procedure to avoid another job. This same fumbling method is used by the student who thinks, "When I finish this boring

English assignment I have to do history which is no fun either." Continual procrastination becomes a habit which may be difficult to break.

As the normal person puts off the tasks he believes he should be doing, he feels guilty and wishes he had used his time more appropriately. This creates a certain uneasiness, so that he feels he is not living up to his better self. By procrastinating, he usually receives some satisfaction by delaying or partially relieving the immediate pressure but at the expense of a feeling of self-worth.

Nothing can be gained by putting off school work from day to day. Most students find they have to study more than twice as hard to learn material that has been postponed, and retention becomes less efficient. This sort of procrastination usually leads to cramming before tests, a very inefficient method of studying. The material learned is soon forgotten because of the disorderly method of placing it into the thought process under stress.

Students procrastinate in a number

of other ways. Do you have any of the habits described here?

1. One of the most common reasons given for wasting study time is "getting in the mood." Much of this lethargic action can be eliminated by establishing a definite place and time for study.

2. The study partnership affords a means of communication of ideas between two people, but it also offers the disadvantage of dependency and the possibility of wasting a great deal of time. Too often, the social aspects of being together become more important than relating information to each other.

3. Many students find ways of avoiding the task of studying by going through various rituals: the "personal ritual" for a boy may involve reading the newspaper, taking time for a smoke, taking off his coat, rolling up his sleeves; a girl may pin up her hair, write her boyfriend's name a number of times, or talk on the phone.

4. "The stomach ritual" requires that students fill their stomachs before and during study, and is also used as a means of encouraging a break. This ritual can go on for hours.

5. The "friendship ritual" is often used by those who feel that even if they can't be good students they can make friends. Anyone within talking

distance qualifies; if the phone is handy, a lengthy call is made to "really exchange ideas."

The Study Environment

The improvement of the study environment is basic to the improvement of study habits. At one time, the author had lectured to his classes on the ideal surroundings for doing schoolwork and had carefully outlined the right and wrong ways to study. He then made a survey of how his students were actually studying. He found that some were doing the major part of their studying between classes, some on the bus or in the car going to and from school, some at home in the living room where their parents watched television, and some in various other confusing situations. Although the ideal cannot always be achieved, all available resources should be utilized to make the actual conditions highly conducive to studying and remembering.

The ideal room for studying is one which is warm, restful, sunny in the daytime, and well-lighted at night. The desk or table should be placed against the wall and close to a window where additional sunlight and air is available. The desk itself should be neat and should have all the equipment necessary for study easily available. The chair should be comfortable and should permit correct posture for sitting and writing. The study desk and chair should be used for no other purpose but study; only materials for doing schoolwork should be kept in this spot. The student should become so accustomed to this atmosphere in this particular place that as soon as he sits down he automatically begins to study.

A student may take these suggestions to the extreme. He may feel that a restful environment means a chair in which he can lean back or a davenport on which to lie. Having achieved this relaxed environment, he finds that not holding up the book would be less discomforting. Then, closing his eyes would shut out distractions. This, of course, brings him to a completely re-laxed state but not to a creative environment for learning. Somewhere between this very restful atmosphere and the uncomfortable, punishment-type of environment is the best situation for learning.

Some students feel that having the television on does not affect their studying. However, it becomes evident to most that there are two visual stimuli: one the television, the other the book. With the radio, there is a similar situation. The radio presents an auditory stimulus versus the visual stimulus of the book.

Other students feel they can absorb more information from a book if there is soft music playing. This may be true if there is considerable disturbance from the outside. However, if there is no other significant disturbance, the big distraction seems to be due to the announcer rather than the music. This lack of variation of attention is not conducive to good concentration.

Most students seem to prefer a quiet atmosphere for study. In an informal survey made by the author of 165 students, 43 per cent stated that they considered being *alone* in a *quiet room* to be their most important aid to learning. However, strange as it may seem, students in *soundproof* rooms find it difficult to study.

Ways to Improve Learning

There is no easy road to learning, but some avenues are better paved and more direct than others. Some study suggestions which have been found to increase the speed of learning and the ability to retain are:

1. Plan to overlearn. Overlearning is learning beyond the point at which the material can just be reproduced. This additional learning pays dividends at reviewing and exam time. Overlearning prevents confusion and builds greater self-confidence.

2. Attack the assignment vigorously. Make contact with the material through as many sense avenues as possible. A half-hearted tackle does not make a good football player or a good student. A simple formula for effective learning is "see it, say it, hear it, do it."

3. Watch for stagnation periods in learning. When one undertakes the study of a new subject, such as French or chemistry, learning follows a fairly characteristic course. As the subject matter becomes more difficult, a period of no progress is often encountered, and the student feels he is making no gain. These periods in which performance is not bettered are called plateaus, but progress goes forward again after the leveling-off period.

4. Start with the difficult studies first. A fresh mind finds it easier to make associations with the material already learned. Subjects that are easiest should usually be left for last since making associations will not require severe concentration.

5. Use little bits of free time to advantage. Carry small cards containing information such as the vocabulary for a foreign language, words that you have looked up in the dictionary the previous day, or words related to concepts or ideas in a specific subject. Glancing at these notes in free moments will keep ideas fresh and active and utilize time that might otherwise be wasted.

6. Review the previous day's lesson before the class period begins. This helps to fix in mind the points already learned and to form the bridge for the next assignment.

7. Be on time to class. Quite often at the very beginning of the period, an important point is discussed or a clue is given which will help in studying or understanding the assignment.

8. Try to arrange for some study time after a class whenever possible. This has certain advantages:

   a. Ideas and explanations that were given in class are still fresh in your mind.

   b. Class notes can be easily rewritten, if necessary.

   c. There is a tendency to want to continue what you were doing.

   d. There is a release of emotional strain after class that may be beneficial to your participation in the work of that class.

9. Summarize the material in your own words. This makes it a part of you. The person who says, "I know it, but I can't say it," does not know it. Until an idea can be integrated and used to develop other ideas, it is worthless. It does not make much difference what a person has read or how many pages of the book he has covered; real education comes from his ability to utilize ideas and express himself.

10. In studying of any kind, time is a variable. The amount of time spent studying depends upon the kind of job the student wants to do, the kind of person he is, his personal feelings about the work itself, and the quality of the end product he wishes to produce in himself.

SOAP

LEARNING NEW MATERIAL

When approaching new subject matter, one should have a calm, collected, and exploratory attitude. Work for success in understanding. There should be no anxiety or tension over not being able to grasp all the variations at the onset. It takes time to think over and try out new ideas.

A successful method for learning new material was worked out during World War II. At that time, it became very important for industry to train a great number of people quickly and efficiently. They had the problem of producing teachers from foremen and others of a similar caliber within the industrial structure. The training program described here was worked out and used with tremendous success.

This process could actually be very useful to the student trying to learn some new procedure, concept, or activity. Study this program carefully, first from the viewpoint of how the task is presented to you, and then how you can present the task to yourself.

Even though you are not always able to set up your learning procedures in a nice four-step program, perhaps you can develop the ability to be your own best teacher. If you can, you will be able to remember more details and have more insight into any job you are faced with, whether it is a problem of motor skill like learning to bowl, or a mental task like working out an algebra assignment.

How does this program apply to English, social studies, and other courses? Present the assignment to *YOU*, the student, in four steps. Be sure you understand the purposes behind each step. The assignment in social studies, for instance, will be made more informative if you take the time

THE FOUR-STEP TRAINING PROGRAM

Step	Purpose	How Accomplished
1. **Prepare the learner**	A. To relieve tension.	A. Put him at ease.
	B. To establish training base.	B. Find out what he already knows about task.
	C. To arouse interest.	C. Tell relation of task to mission.
	D. To give him confidence.	D. Tie task to his experience.
2. **Present the task**	A. To make sure he understands what to do and why.	A. Tell, show, illustrate, question, carefully and patiently, use task analysis.
	B. To insure retention.	B. Stress key points.
	C. To avoid giving him more than he can grasp.	C. Instruct clearly and completely, one step at a time.
3. **Try out learner's performance**	A. To be sure he has right method.	A. Have him perform the task.
	B. To prevent wrong habit forming.	B. Correct errors immediately.
	C. To be sure he knows what he is doing and why.	C. Have him tell and show you and explain key points to you.
	D. To test his knowledge.	D. Ask questions.
	E. To avoid putting him on the job prematurely.	E. Continue until you know that he knows.
4. **Follow-up**	A. To give him confidence.	A. Put him on his own; praise as fitting.
	B. To be sure he takes no chances, and knows he is not left alone.	B. Encourage questions; tell him where he can get help.
	C. To be sure he stays on the beam.	C. Check frequently at first.
	D. To show your confidence in him.	D. Gradually reduce amount of checking.

and make the effort to follow through on each step, especially the second one—"Present the task"; be sure you "understand what to do and why" by telling, showing, illustrating, questioning, and analyzing the task carefully.

The method has been successfully used in a number of learning situations. It has been changed and revised since the original presentation but is essentially the same.

The aids to learning which have just been discussed have been suggested by authorities in the fields of psychology and learning as being sound and effective. The suggestions which follow have been made by students for improvement of schoolwork:

1. Homework grades can be improved by doing two simple things—writing down the complete assignment accurately, and starting to work on a new assignment as soon after the class period as possible. The sooner this is done the fewer the details that will be forgotten.

2. Notebooks and outside reading should be kept current by being worked on every day. Thus, projects are kept from becoming too large to handle comfortably. This also helps to eliminate panic as the deadline approaches.

3. As an assignment is read, jotting down the main thought of each paragraph or making a brief note about it helps one to remember and provides valuable review material.

4. Having a dictionary handy when studying results in better understanding of the material since unfamiliar words can easily be looked up as they occur.

5. Taking a short break between study sessions is restful and relaxing. Walking around the room and stretching increases blood circulation which helps to produce a body tone more receptive to studying.

6. Participation in class discussion is a valuable way to understand and become involved in material as it is being presented. Other class members can benefit when constructive questions are asked which clarify obscure points.

7. A subject often takes time to become interesting. Most people find that as they become familiar with a subject by working with it, the material offers a satisfactory challenge. Most courses do not create an immediate, spontaneous, joyous response in students.

8. It is a waste of time to wonder how many pages a report should contain to impress the instructor. Instead the student should ask himself how much he wants to add to his knowledge. The answer should determine the length of the assignment for him.

9. When tests are returned, analyze the questions missed; discussing the entire test with another student is a help to learning and an aid in finding the points which should receive special emphasis.

10. Work hard. Little effort produces little results. Get with it!

RECOMMENDED METHODS OF STUDY

In the previous section, general aids for the improvement of study have been presented. In addition to these aids there are formulas for studying that have been found effective. They are referred to as "formulas" because they offer definite procedures to follow. A number of study methods are presented here because the effectiveness of different study procedures varies with different students. One or more of them might be right for you.

The P-A-T Method
(Previewing—Attacking—Testing)

A. Previewing.

1. Skim quickly through the assignment; note headings, pictures, graphs,

tables, and the first sentence of each paragraph.

2. Carefully read the beginning and ending paragraphs of the assignment, paying special attention to the topic sentences. (The topic sentence is the central thought of a paragraph usually, but not always, the first sentence.)

3. If there are questions at the beginning or end of the assigned material, look them over quickly.

B. Attacking.

1. Read actively: do something to fix the material in your mind. Underline, make marginal notes, outline the paragraphs, or use whatever method is effective for *you* in learning.

C. Testing.

1. Ask yourself questions which might be similar to possible test questions.

2. Get together with several students and take turns asking questions.

3. Answer the questions in the text.

4. Reread the parts of the assignment which the testing has shown you do not understand.

The Survey Q3R Method [1]

This system is similar to P-A-T. The formula is: survey, question, read, recite, review.

The Study—Rest—Study—Rest Method

This method is useful for long study periods. It is quite effective in helping material to be absorbed and giving it a chance to "soak in." Although no special length of time is suggested for the study period, most students find that at least 45 minutes is necessary to really get an assignment organized.

The rest periods can be much shorter; even a few minutes of relaxation and stretching may produce the desired effect and increase efficiency. It is usually restful to change the study activity—for instance, a change from piano practice to a math assignment or from typing an English paper to an art project.

The Question and Answer Method

In this system of study, a question is written on one side of a 3 x 5 card and an answer on the other side. As each question is answered, the card is turned over to see if the correct answer was given. This method can be used at any time or place simply by carrying 3 x 5 cards in one's pocket. It is a great help in learning and memorizing, and test questions can be anticipated.

The Outline Method

Briefly outlining a chapter as it is being read helps in memorization and brings about more thorough reading. The Outline Method can be used with any subject. It is a valuable aid in picking out the most important thoughts in a chapter. A more thorough discussion of textbook outlining as well as general outlining procedures will be found in Chapter 7.

Diagram Method

Although the "Diagram Method" is not a complete study formula, it is helpful when used with other study methods. Diagrams can be effective in identifying and remembering important points. Both reading and lecture notes may be improved by an occasional diagram to clarify ideas and group related facts. For example, a simple diagram of the P-A-T Method might help you to understand it better:

The Five Step Study Plan

Step 1—The Once Over.

Make a short 4- or 5-minute preview of the assignment. Thumb carefully through the assigned pages. Note topic sentences; read the first sentence of each paragraph and the summary paragraph intensely. Try to grasp the general idea of the material.

Step 2—Who? What? Why? When? How? Build Some Curiosity About Your Material.

Make up a few questions as you glance through the material, so your reading has purpose. Keep these questions in the back of your mind to help you become aware of what you are trying to get from your reading.

Step 3—Read and Remember.

Now read the lesson from beginning to end. Mentally note the answers to the questions you have asked when you come to them. Give special emphasis to other important material you did not question before. When you read, notice the way the author has organized the material. Understand what HE feels is important.

Step 4—Think—Talk It Over.

As soon as the whole lesson is finished, glance back at each paragraph or subtopic and state what it contained. Continue, perhaps making a few notations, until the whole lesson has been covered.

Step 5—Test—Has Your Reading Left an Impression?

Later, perhaps the next day or before the class meets, test your memory by repeating the concepts and ideas. If details have been forgotten, read to refresh. You are now ready for an examination.

Another Study Method

The final study approach to be given here has been used successfully by some students. Like the others, it may not necessarily be the best technique for *you* nor may it be the best one to use for every subject:

1. Read the overview or summary first to get the basic subject matter.

2. Read and underline the most important phrases in each subtopic.

3. Go back and concentrate on these high spots.

4. Speed-read the whole thing.

5. Put it away for awhile.

6. Review it later.

SUMMARY

Analyzing the above systems of learning new material will show that the general formula seems to be:

1. Get an overview.

2. Go back and study—by outlining,

underlining, rereading parts, or whatever method might be the most effective to get the material clearly in mind.
It should be remembered that most
people are unable to scan material and
feel that they have studied it.

3. Summarize, analyze, test, clarify,
and crystallize ideas.

Do you have a favorite "formula"
for studying? Perhaps you have never
analyzed your study methods. In the
space below, write the steps you use
when you sit down to study.

_____

_____

_____

_____

_____

_____

_____

Do you think your study formula can

be improved? List here the points you
feel need changing.

_____

_____

_____

_____

_____

_____

_____

Now that you have analyzed your
study techniques, you can develop one
which will be the most helpful to you.
Perhaps you feel that one of the formulas suggested in this chapter will be
best for you. Write out the method
you decide to adopt, then make a diagram of it so you can be sure of the
main points.

Reference

1. Francis P. Robinson, *Effective Study*,
New York, Harper and Brothers, 1961,
pp. 13–49.

4

COMPREHENSION OF WORDS

UNDERSTANDING WORDS

Language, both spoken and written, has always played a tremendous part in the lives of human beings. At the present time, language is emphasized more than ever before as a means of influencing and controlling the minds and actions of individuals and nations. Therefore, it is very important that we learn to use words carefully and to read with comprehension.

When we speak or write, we want to communicate our thoughts and ideas to others as accurately as possible. In order to achieve this precise communication, we must be aware of two overlapping but separate aspects of words—*denotation* and *connotation*.

Denotation is what a word stands for and points to; it is often called the "dictionary meaning." The connotation of a word refers to the overtones, meanings, and values that are implied or suggested rather than expressed in the denotative meaning. These two important word qualities are enlarged upon in the sections which follow.

Denotation

Because words stand for many different kinds of things, they are called *symbols*. The object or class of objects, quality, idea, thought, or situation to which a word refers is its referent (rĕf′erent); a word gets its basic meaning, or denotation, by symbolizing or representing this referent.

We can see that meaning is not in the word itself but in whatever it refers to. For example, words such as

"screen," "play," and "trap." A screen may be, among other things, a movable partition, a surface for showing motion pictures, a wire mesh, or a sieve. What a word refers to is generally clear from its context—that is, the words around it or the way it is used at a particular time.

The definiteness of word meanings depends partly on how exactly a word brings to mind a particular referent. Words may be *concrete* or *abstract;* each of these types expresses a different degree of definiteness.

Concrete words are the most definite because they refer to actual objects. "Table," for instance, has a definite meaning; although several people hearing the word may think of different kinds of tables, the basic meaning of a piece of furniture with a flat top and four legs remains fairly constant.

Abstract words are difficult to use accurately, because they do not have specific referents. "United States" may refer to a group of people, a land area, a government, a certain way of life, or to all these things together. Such words as "beauty," "evil," "art," or "education" do not mean the same things to everyone. When abstract words are used in speaking or writing, they should be explained by the use of concrete words and, when possible, by concrete examples.

Connotation

The full meaning of most words cannot be given by a dictionary, because a standard definition cannot indicate the many possible shadings of meanings. Many related words (synonyms) have the same basic denotation, but because each has a different *connotation,* they cannot be used interchangeably.

Consider the terms "man's best friend," "canine," and "cur." Essentially, all three refer to a dog. But what does "man's best friend" make you think of? Naturally, a pet, a friendly companion. "Canine" has an impersonal, scientific sound and could refer to any member of the dog family, including the wolf and jackal; "cur" brings to mind a snarling, worthless animal. In consulting a dictionary for synonyms, you must be careful to

choose the one expressing exactly what you want to say.

The connotation of words reflects certain attitudes or emotions of the person using them. A similar feeling is usually aroused in his listeners or readers. These suggested qualities of words are affected by the context in which they are used and the general attitude of society toward the people who use them (teachers, politicians, gangsters, adolescents, ministers, etc.).

Whether we intend to or not, we express the way we feel about the world through the connotations of the words we use. There are not many words that may be considered "neutral"— that is, with relatively few overtones to color the basic meanings. Even these neutral words assume various shadings of meanings in certain contexts and when they are used by people in whom they arouse strong feelings.

Compare these two lists:

Words with Overtones	Words That Are More Neutral
bureaucrat	government official
drunkard	alcoholic
peasant	farmer
speculation	investment
jailbird	prisoner
cop	peace officer
vicious	antisocial
politician	statesman
pedagogue	teacher

Importance of Denotation and Connotation

The study of denotation can help build a vocabulary which contains many concrete words. This is of great value in improving the effectiveness of both verbal and written communication. When you speak and write clearly in carefully chosen, concrete terms, you avoid confusing yourself and others.

At the same time, being sensitive to connotations will help you express your feelings better and will make you more aware of what others feel. Reading is more enjoyable when you can appreciate the ways in which connotation is used to arouse certain emotions and form pictures. This awareness will also help protect you from being easily influenced by persuasive words.

LEARNING FROM READING

The rate of learning from reading depends upon how quickly associations are formed between already known material and the material being studied.

Poor readers are "word" readers; they read individual words rather than thought units because they cannot make associations quickly enough and are not reading with the idea of making bigger over-all associations. Also, they are not fitting concepts to self, which is the basic utilization of the ideas presented from the outside source.

However, one cannot grasp thoughts without understanding words; to try to do this is to distort or lose the main purpose of the study period. Remember, studying is not reading a book to see how fast it can be finished. It is a way of learning by assimilating ideas which are understood through words. The understanding obtained from the material depends on the ability of the thought process to grasp a concept in context and then to file it with other information in the mental storehouse.

Basically, then, the problem of learning from reading resolves itself into getting the greatest number of concepts in the shortest length of time. The faster one can read and grasp ideas, the better chance he has for success. In order to understand ideas, it is necessary to understand the words making up the ideas. The larger the vocabulary of the individual, the less often will it be necessary for him to consult the dictionary.

BUILDING A VOCABULARY

Everyone possesses both a *recognition* vocabulary and a *speaking-writing* vocabulary. The recognition vocabulary consists of the words recognized and understood when they are read or heard but which are not generally used (pulchritude; troubadour; tertiary). The speaking-writing vocabulary includes the words commonly used in writing and talking.

A vocabulary consisting only of essential words ordinarily used in everyday living would be limited and repetitious. The recognition vocabulary is increased through reading, and this, in turn, increases the number of words available to the speaking–writing vocabulary. The recognition vocabulary is about three times larger than the spoken vocabulary because of the many new words added from reading, often through context.

Words can become friends when they are investigated and the interesting substance is discovered beneath their surface meanings. For instance,

the word "ammonia" is derived from *Ammon,* the Egyptian sun god, near whose shrine in Libya the salt (sal ammoniac) was first obtained.

"Assassin" comes from the Arabic word *hashish,* a narcotic made from Indian hemp. The original assassins were members of a secret order during the Crusades, who intoxicated themselves with hashish before setting out on their missions of murder. The literal meaning of assassin was "eaters of hashish."

The word "blizzard" came into general use in the United States in the severe winter of 1880–1881. Blizzard is believed to have sprung from an English offshoot of *blaze*–"to blow."

Shading of meanings (connotations) make words as interesting as characters in a book. Interest in words can lead a student to want to apply them in writing or speaking with the precision of a draftsman or skilled technician. By the inclusion of fine details, he can give his finished product polish and distinction.

The standard advice for vocabulary building given to students is to look up in the dictionary each new word as it is encountered. The only drawback to this method is that the continuity of thought may be lost if reading is constantly interrupted.

It may be better to look up only those words which are completely unfamiliar and to try to understand the others from context. Some students find that placing a check mark ($\sqrt{}$) after a new word identifies it so it can be looked up later and allows them to maintain the flow of thought.

It is a fact that words are better understood in context than through parrot memorization. It is of little value for a student to memorize a certain number of words each day so he can say he has increased his vocabulary. Actually, he is looking through

the wrong end of the telescope. It is more important that he have an understanding of the meanings of the words in context; he should develop an inner feeling for words rather than a surface vocabulary that quickly peels off with disuse.

Becoming familiar with word roots, prefixes and suffixes will help in recognizing many words from context. The basic part of a word is the *root*. *Prefixes* (syllables placed in front of the root) and *suffixes* (syllables placed after the root) modify its meaning.

English is made up largely of words derived from the Anglo-Saxon, Greek, and Latin languages. Knowing the meanings of some of these commonly used roots, prefixes, and suffixes will help in the understanding of new words and clarify the meaning of many old ones. Building a vocabulary by memorizing these word elements has the same advantages as memorizing multiplication tables for quickly working with numbers.

Prefixes, roots, and suffixes may be thought of as clues to word understanding. The following lists may help in learning a number of these clues in a short time. (It is a good idea to carry a 3 x 5 card filled with some of them for easy reference and memorization.)

WORD ROOTS

Root	Meaning	Examples
ambul	walk	*ambul*ate, *ambul*ant
ann(u)	year	*annu*al, *annu*ity
arch	principal, chief; original	*arch*bishop, *arch*etype

WORD ROOTS (Continued)

Root	Meaning	Examples
aur, aud, audio	ear	*aur*al, *aud*ience
auto	self	*auto*graph, *auto*mobile
brachi	arm	*brachi*ate, *brace*let
cal, calor	to be warm, heat	*calor*ie, *calor*imeter
craft	skill, art, trade	wood*craft*, handi*craft*
dorm	sleep	*dorm*ant, *dorm*itory
feder	league	*feder*ation, *feder*alism
fili	son or daughter; associated	*fili*al, af*fili*ate
lav, lavat	wash	*lav*e, *lavat*ory
macro	large, excessive	*macro*scopic, *macro*physics
mal	bad, defective, ill	*mal*practice, *mal*adjusted
micro	very small	*micro*scopic, *micro*be
met(e)r	measure	speed*ometer*, *metr*ic
psych(o)	mind, soul, spirit	*psych*ic, *psycho*analyze
tract	draw, drag	de*tract*, pro*tract*
vac(u), vaca(t)	be empty; free	*vacu*ous, *vaca*tion
vid, vis	see	*vid*eo, *vis*ibility

PREFIXES
(Arranged by general meanings)

Prefix	Meaning	Examples
For		
ad-	addition; direction	*ad*ditive, *ad*joining
pro-	in favor of; advance	*pro*-British, *pro*ceed
Against		
ab-	not; draw from	*ab*normal, *ab*stract
anti-	against; reverse of	*anti*body, *anti*climax
contra-	opposing	*contra*diction
il-, im-, in-, ir-, non-, un-	not	*il*logical, *ir*replaceable
Above		
hyper-	excessive; exaggerated	*hyper*bole
super-	superior; beyond	*super*man
supra-	above (location)	*supra*orbital
Below		
hypo-	under; less than	*hypo*thyroidism
*sub*normal	infra-	below, beneath
*under*estimate, *under*dog	sub-	beneath; a lower order
*infra*costal	under-	beneath; subordinate

PREFIXES (Continued)
(Arranged by general meanings)

Prefix	Meaning	Examples
Assemble		
amphi-	on all sides; around	*amphi*theater
circum-	movement around	*circum*navigate
com-	jointly	*com*mingle
hetero-	unlike	*hetero*geneous
inter-	between; among	*inter*action
juxta-	near, beside	*juxta*position
proto-	first; in front of	*proto*type
trans-	across; beyond	*trans*port, *trans*cend
para-	aside; beyond	*para*phrase
Divide		
de-	away from, separate	*de*compose
dis-	asunder, apart	*dis*agree
mis-	wrong	*mis*calculate
re-	repeat; go back	*re*animate, *re*coil
se-	withdraw	*se*cede
Within		
co-, col-, com-, con-	together, accompanying; joint action	*co*heir, *co*operate, *col*linear
en-, endo-l	into, inside	*en*circle
il-, im-, in-, ir-	into, toward; in, inward	*im*migrate, *in*come, *ir*radiate
intra-, intros-	within, directed inward	*intra*mural, *intro*spection
sy-, syl-, sym-, syn-, sys-	(same function as prefix co-)	*syl*labicate *sys*tem
Without		
a-	lacking	*a*pathetic
ec-, ecto-	outer, external	*ecto*parasite
ex-	from, out of	*ex*ample
Amount		
ambi-	both sides	*ambi*dextrous
di-	twice, double	*di*chromatic
extra-	besides, beyond	*extra*sensory
hemi-	half	*hemi*sphere
iso-	equal	*iso*metric
mon-, mono-	single, one alone	*mon*arch, *mono*logue
multi-	much, many	*multi*cellular
pan-, panto-	all	*pan*demic

PREFIXES (*Continued*)
(Arranged by general meanings)

Prefix	Meaning	Examples
Amount		
poly-	much, many	*poly*chrome
semi-	half, partly	*semi*precious
ultra-	beyond, excessive	*ultra*conventional
Time		
ante-	before (in space or time)	*ante*date
neo-	new, recent	*neo*classic
post-	later, after	*post*script
pre-	before, prior to	*pre*historic
retro-	backward (in space or time)	*retro*gress
Space		
dia-	through, across	*dia*meter
omni-	all	*omni*present
Numbers		
bi-	two, twice	*bi*ped, *bi*annual
cent-, centi-	hundred	*centi*gram
kilo-	thousand	*kilo*meter
milli-	thousand (division)	*milli*gram
tri-	three	*tri*angle
uni-	one	*uni*form
State or Condition		
dys-	ill; difficult	*dys*function
eu-	good, well	*eu*phemism
homo-	the same	*homo*geneous
hydro-	water	*hydro*therapy
hypno-	sleep	*hypno*therapy
miso-	hatred of	*miso*gamy
ortho-	straight, correct	*ortho*dox
pneumo-	lungs, respiration	*pneumo*bacillus
pseudo-	false, pretended	*pseudo*nym
stereo-	solid, hard	*stereo*gram
thermo-	heat, warmth	*thermo*nuclear

SUFFIXES

Suffix	Meaning	Examples
-able, -ible	capable of being	access*ible*, attain*able*
-ad	denoting a collection of a certain number	tri*ad*
-al	of, or pertaining to	feud*al*
-an	belonging to, a member of	republic*an*
-ar	pertaining to or connected with	cell*ar*
-ate	office, body of officers	consul*ate*
-ectomy	surgical removal	thyroid*ectomy*
-ee	affected by or the object of some action	assign*ee*
-eer	concerned with, or engaged in	mountain*eer*
-eous, -ious, -ous	having, full of	aqu*eous*, volumin*ous*
-er, -or	one who performs an action	deceiv*er*
-escent	beginning to be	adol*escent*
-et, -ette	diminutive	lanc*et*, cigar*ette*
-fy, -ify	to make, to cause to be	lique*fy*
-gen	produced or growing	endo*gen*
-geny	origin	phylo*geny*
-gram, -graph	written or drawn record	cable*gram*, mimeo*graph*
-iatric, -iatry	pertaining to a physician or medicine, medical care	psych*iatric*, psych*iatry*
-ic, ical	pertaining or belonging to	bas*ic*, alphabet*ical*
-ist	one who is concerned with something or holds certain principles	real*ist*
-ite	associated with a place, doctrine, etc.	Israel*ite*
-itis	denoting inflammation of a part or organ	bronch*itis*
-ize	following a line of action, acting toward or upon	econom*ize*, bapt*ize*
-ment	act or process of	move*ment*
-or	state, quality	err*or*, val*or*
-ory	having the nature of; a place or thing for	commendat*ory*, direct*ory*
-osis	action, process, condition	metamorph*osis*
-phobia	fear, dread, hatred	agora*phobia*
-scope	instrument for viewing	chrono*scope*
-tion	action or condition	commisera*tion*

PHONETICS

Although there is considerable controversy about utilizing phonetics (speech sounds and their production) for reading improvement, it should receive serious consideration. Often, students will either transpose letters or not read the sounds of the letters correctly, and they will get an entirely different idea from two words that may appear somewhat alike. For example, many students will become confused with the words "immortality" and "immorality." However, perceiving the sounds in sequence may help to give understanding of the word.

There is some evidence that on both high school and college levels reading achievement is related to phonetics. It has been found important in the reading and learning process to have the ability to hear sounds distinctly and to discriminate between similar sounds. In addition, it is necessary to interpret visual symbols into correct sounds which form the words which transmit the thought.

Many students can recognize arrangements of letters and transform them into sounds. Reading, then, becomes a matter of being visually receptive to the letters and being able to perceive them visually and orally. Thus, the eye, ear, and speech are being used together to form a complete understanding of the word.

Of course, reading is much more than the recognizing of sounds; it is a complex system of grouping letters together to symbolize words in order to make ideas communicable with or without oral pronunciation. However, if a person does not have the ability to recognize sounds in words, he does not have the ability to comprehend, because part of meaning comes from this conception. The work of Alice M. Cottrell and Grace M. Brown [1] indicates that there is a high relationship between low phonetic ability and not being a good reader. Poor readers may not always be phonetically handicapped, but the phonetically handicapped reader is likely to be a poor reader because he will not obtain meaning from the words.

Some students have gone through school without having been taught the phonetic rules. This is partly due to the fact that young children in the early grades are often confused by too many exceptions to the rules for making the sounds of letters comprising words. Some of the most common words are non-phonetic. For instance, according to phonetic rules, "one" should sound like "own," "are" like "air," "come" like "comb." In spite of these common words having a special sound of their own, there are many words that definitely follow the phonetic pattern. Consequently, a person having a knowledge of phonetics can more easily understand what he reads.

For example, most of the consonants maintain their basic sounds, especially at the beginning of words. See if you are able to correctly pronounce these sounds:

v x b n g o e t d j k y p
i r q s a l f c m w u z h

gr fl   sw ch sm cl tr sk tw
gl wh dr pl st   fr br sh th

There are other letters, especially the vowels, in which there are a few variations of the most common sounds. For example, long "ē" (need), and short "ĕ" (red), long "ā" (ape) and short "ă" (at), long "ī" (pie), and short "ĭ" (it). These letters being capable of sound variation must be used with flexibility in the mind of the reader.

Reading speed can be increased when the sound and sight of a word becomes more familiar. With this integration, it becomes less important to produce sounds vocally or even subvocally to understand the word. This, in turn, eliminates the need to move the lips or to go through the process of producing any kind of verbalization. Lip movement, being slower than eye movement, slows down the speed of reading.

To improve reading speed it is necessary not to read and pronounce individual words but instead to grasp thoughts. Pronounce these syllables so their sounds will be familiar to you as they occur in words you read.

ang	ing	teen	tean
erg	ton	tone	ingle
ish	ler	ible	able
bel	lous	ious	angle
edge	can	tion	sion

There is no question that the above clues are reading aids, but phonetics has its traps. That is why many schools have felt that this type of confusion should not be added to all the other problems involved in learning, especially at the beginning stage. Now you should be old enough to recognize the confusing elements in the phonetic method and make good use of some specific phonetic aids.

Using phonetic clues to pronounce the following words may create some confusion. However, past experience has taught us that there are variations in the sounds of letters (like "w") or letter grouping (like "ough").

tough	thought	through	threw
sword	swim	wren	mould
would	wool	wood	mood

A particular tool, such as a hammer, a screwdriver, or a pair of pliers may not be useful for every kind of work and may even be a hindrance in certain jobs. This does not mean it should be discarded for all jobs. One must know when each tool would be useful. This is true of tools used in reading. Phonetics are useful under certain conditions. See if you can apply phonetic principles to the following:

ane	ene	ine	une
ale	ele	ile	ule
ur	ir	er	ar
ooph	uf	upe	op
aud	awd	ud	aid
oud	oid	oys	oat

Basically, phonetics is an aid in transferring meaning from vocal sounds made when one looks at letters or groups of letters. These sounds then form words which take on meaning from having been heard. Since we have two vocabularies—vocal and visual—we gain understanding of concepts through one or another of these areas and sometimes through both.

Reference

1. Alice M. Cottrell and Grace M. Brown, "Report of the Phonetic Analysis of College Freshmen," Consulting Psychologist Press, Inc., Palo Alto, California.

Test Yourself on Chapter 4

Place the letter of the correct definition beside each word.
(You will find the key to this test after the last exercise.)

Abstract	—	A. The literal meaning of "assassin."
Referent	—	B. Speech sounds and their production.
Root	—	C. Vocabulary consisting of words used in daily life.
Recognition	—	D. Syllables placed before the root.
Suffix	—	E. The "dictionary meaning" of a word.
Speaking-Writing	—	F. That to which a word refers.
Context	—	G. Words with few overtones.
Prefix	—	H. The implied meaning of a word.
Phonetics	—	I. Words that do not refer to specific things.
Denotation	—	J. Words with Latin derivations.
Concrete	—	K. Syllables placed after the root.
Neutral	—	L. Words.
Connotation	—	M. The setting in which a word is used.
Symbols	—	N. The basic part of a word.
		O. Words that refer to actual objects.
		P. Vocabulary consisting of words understood when read but not generally used.

Vocabulary Exercises

A. Make two personal vocabulary lists, each one containing at least ten words; one should consist of words from your *recognition* vocabulary and the other of words from your *speaking-writing* vocabulary. Place a star (*) in front of any new words you've read or used in the last week.

Recognition Vocabulary	**Speaking-Writing Vocabulary**

B. It is possible that you have never spoken aloud some of the words in your recognition vocabulary. You can increase your oral vocabulary by being certain of the meanings and pronunciation of such words and by *using* them. Follow these steps:

1. Make a list of the words you have never really used, be sure to include any new words from exercise A. Find their meanings and pronunciations in your dictionary and mark each word for pronunciation. *Say each word aloud.*

Word	Meaning	Pronunciation

2. Make up sentences including each word from the above list.

3. Make a special effort to use the words in conversation or in class or at any appropriate opportunity. It might help you to think of a proper time for using each of these new words. Utilize this space for making such notes. Remember, each time you say the words and gain confidence in their use, they really become part of your speaking-writing vocabulary.

C. Write down the ideas that come to your mind as you read each of the following words. Then consult your dictionary to find "neutral" synonyms for them. Write the synonym under each word. Do you find differences between your feelings about these terms and the "dictionary" meanings of the synonyms?

1. prohibition	3. propaganda	5. shyster	7. fraternize
_____	_____	_____	_____
2. hermit	4. insane	6. stingy	8. liar
_____	_____	_____	_____

D. Using your dictionary, find the derivations (Latin, Greek, etc.) of the words below, and write the definitions. Several examples are given. Then start a list of your own composed of new words you encounter in your course work and want to understand better.

Word	Derivation	Definition
companion	L. *com*, with + *panis*, bread	A person who associates with another; comrade. Literally, *bread fellow*.
disturb	L. *dis*, apart + *turbare*, to disorder	To break up or agitate what is quiet
divine		
adjourn		
immaculate		
hemoglobin		
dynamometer		
plebiscite		
sculpture		
servomechanism		

Key to Self-test

I, F, N, P, K, C, M, D, B, E, O, G, H, L

5

READING IMPROVEMENT

PHYSICAL EFFICIENCY IN READING

Reading involves physical activity and is dependent upon many physiological factors. One of these factors is the functioning of the visual system. The eye must focus upon printed words, which are relatively small; visual defects, even though they may not be serious enough to cause conspicuous errors in reading, can cause chronic eyestrain and make reading difficult and tiring. The extra effort needed to read adequately may cause irritability or a general feeling of tiredness and restlessness.

The defects of the eye which seem to greatly affect reading and may cause fatigue are astigmatism (uneven curvature of the front part of the eye or lens), myopia (nearsightedness), and hyperopia (farsightedness). These conditions may be aided with glasses. Anyone who has headaches or eyeaches from watching movies, doing light reading, or studying for 4 or 5 hours should have his eyes checked for physical defects by a competent eye specialist.

General body fatigue may affect the eyes and thereby lower reading efficiency.[1] Sufficient rest and sleep are very important to keep the body functioning at its best. However, the belief of many students that at least eight and sometimes ten hours of sleep are required for eyes and body to work well is not substantiated scientifically. Although the sleep habits of individual students vary considerably, most of them get more than they actually require for general physical well-being. The eyes need rest, of course, but they can function efficiently for long periods of time without sleep.

Normal exercise is both necessary and beneficial to all muscles of the body, including those controlling the eyes. But eye muscles can become tired under prolonged strain, just as leg muscles become tired from too much walking. Besides defective vision, some causes of eye fatigue are an extraordinary amount of reading or close work of any kind (which keeps the eyes focussed on small areas for a long time), or holding the head and the book in one position for too long.

When muscle strain occurs in any part of the body, a shift of position usually brings relief. Diversion of eye activity, like other types of bodily activity, will help in alleviating strain. Many students find that closing the eyes for a short time and changing the muscle tensions by shifting position in various parts of the body, or by stretching brings effective relief and removes "cobwebs."

An occasional change in the way a book is being held also helps to combat fatigue. If the book has been resting on the arm of a chair for a while, moving to a table for a time will help eliminate tension in the muscles of the neck and hands. It is easier to hold a book steady on a surface such as a desk or table; this simple act may reduce strain on the eyes, neck, and hands.

IMPROVING READING SPEED

Whether one is a student with a stack of textbooks to wade through or an executive with a briefcase full of reports to read, the problem is very much the same: "How can I read faster and more efficiently, and cover more material in a shorter time?" Most students read at a rate of about 300 words a minute. This rate can often be doubled if a genuine effort is made to do so. However, it is important to emphasize that reading speeds must be adjusted to the reading material.

Why is it that a novel can be read and understood faster than a psychology text, but a psychology text can be read faster than a chemistry text or material of a highly scientific nature? The material in a novel presents feelings and emotional situations against a specific background. The changes that take place in the characters and the setting are described in much detail. The reader is invited by the author to experience these changes and identify with the characters, and he moves rapidly from one idea or sequence of events to another.

When you read a novel, you understand and remember many things, not because you are required to, but because you want to. You are under no pressure to remember all or many specific ideas for the purpose of reproducing what you have read, as is the case when a textbook is being read. A novel is written to entertain and is read for enjoyment.

In the writing of psychology or sociology or history, more material is concentrated into a smaller space. Thus, the paragraph becomes quite important, in contrast to the novel, in which the chapter is usually more important. The paragraph in this more compact reading matter contains several ideas and often variations of these ideas. This kind of material requires thought so that both the basic concept and the shadings of meanings will be understood.

If you are able to read concepts and groups of words rather than individual words, you are able to move right along the page from one idea to another. However, the reading of chemistry, physics, or mathematics texts is slower because it is harder to find previously known material with which to make as-

sociations. In other words, when you are able to look at a large number of words and make an association quickly, you can read faster. When it takes a while to mentally shuffle background knowledge in order to make an association with the words being read, then, of course, reading is slowed down. The concepts presented in a novel do not produce much strain for the reader in making associations because they are related to many of his personal experiences. But when chemistry is being read, it is often necessary to "think" in order to find a relationship between the new idea and the known informa-

tion and related experiences of the reader.

Improving Speed and Comprehension

What appears to be slow reading may actually be the *rereading* of certain words which involves the movement of the eyes forward and back over the same area. Forcing oneself to read through all kinds of reading matter without repeating, and reading by thought units or idea units rather than words will be of great help in improving reading speed. Although the reading rate for works of a scientific nature may not match that for easier material, it too can be greatly improved.

Psychologists agree that seeing, like playing the piano, speaking a foreign language, or playing golf, is a skill that must be learned. The eyes move like a pianist's fingers and can be taught to perform with as much dexterity as other parts of the body.

The eye can be trained to see faster. Many students have been helped to see more in a shorter time by practicing with flash cards or a tachistoscope (a

mechanical device which exposes a word or phrase for a fraction of a second). Words that may at first require a half-second of exposure to be recognized can, after practice, be seen in $\frac{1}{100}$ or $\frac{1}{500}$ of a second. The number of figures that can be seen and reproduced can also be greatly increased with training.

The average person, as he goes through the printed page, reads "word, word, word, word." In so doing, his eyes are alternately fixating and moving, fixating and moving, as he goes along. It is while the eyes are stopped that one can see and comprehend. The way to read more effectively is to learn to use larger spanning movements and fewer fixations.

Eyes can be taught to grasp a greater number of words. Instead of reading this material as you see it with the dots under it, you can read it from thought units by following the various phrases. Thus you can see a greater expanse of material in one exposure. By spanning a greater amount in a fixation, you have fewer stops, consequently faster reading, and ideas are put into the thought process faster than words. By reading in this manner, both speed and comprehension are increased. Start now to train your eyes to see larger areas faster. Break old habits and establish new ones. You will find your greater efficiency will bring new satisfactions in reading and learning.

This exercise will help you train yourself to move your eyes across the page in three jumps. Notice how much meaning is derived from the three key words in the eye span.

eyes	can	see
lots	more	space
watch	your	eyes
make	big	sweeps
speed up	your	reading
meaning	comes from	words
comprehension	comes	easily
now	start	looking
wonderful	tourist	attraction
general	sales	ability
better	insurance	service
invest	capital	wisely
improving	classroom	skills
brief	summary	note
panel	discussion	group
family	life	education
broad	viewpoint	understanding
current	community	expansion
widely	different	conditions
largest	farm	population
abundant	medical	facilities

well	known	brand
oil	consumption	rate
during	winter	months
big	city	newspaper
large	volume	correspondence
finest	trout	fishing
carefully	considered	judgments
long	term	gains
preferred	stocks	income
wide	profit	range
future	business	expansion
federal	reserve	system
stable	labor	force

See how well you can do on this reading test in both speed and comprehension. Remember to read by thought units. Mark down the beginning and ending time to find the reading time.

377 words

Beginning Time: Hr: —— Min: —— Sec: ——

Despite the high educational standards and the comparatively low illiteracy rate in America, most people are poor readers. The average college student reads less than 300 words per minute. This is a very wasteful, time-consuming procedure. Slow reading is as inadequate as the "hunt and peck" method of typing. No firm would hire a typist who used this plodding method, yet we plod through reading in the same manner when actually the ability to assimilate material at a high rate of speed may determine the amount of success we may achieve.

Probably the greatest error among students as well as businessmen is that they tend toward perfectionism in their reading, in the fear that they will miss something important. However, the truth is that reading whole thoughts, as phrases, increases both speed and comprehension.

The rapid reader has received no mystic blessing. The way one reads is no more than a habit, which can be good or bad. Most people have ceased to improve their reading skill since about the fourth or fifth grade. Thus, the slow reader has become slow by forming a bad habit, by neglecting to utilize speed in a period of his life when he could train his movements to far exceed those of a ten-year-old child. But to those who are willing to exert the effort required to learn new and better habits, there is the possibility of doubling or even tripling the speed and comprehension with which they read, actually deriving more pleasure and knowledge from their reading because of their transition from a poor visual pattern to one requiring more speed of vision and thought.

If you follow the suggestion made previously, you will find that you will be skimming along with greater speed and will be able to grasp much larger areas of thought. Do not allow yourself to fall back into the old, sluggish patterns. It will take a long time, certainly, to shake yourself completely loose from the old habits; they cannot be changed after a few short paragraphs of the more efficient method. But if you will apply yourself consistently, you will find that your effort has been richly rewarded with greater pleasure and understanding than reading has ever supplied for you before.

Ending Time: Hr: ___ Min: ___ Sec: ___
Reading Time: Min: ___ Sec: ___

If you read this test in one minute, you are going along at the average college speed of about 300 words per minute. If you completed it in 45 seconds, you are above average for material of this level of difficulty. If it took you more than a minute and 45 seconds, you are one of those who would find it to your advantage to develop new reading skills.

Can you answer all these questions correctly? (For answers, see page 71.)

True—False

1. _____Americans are poor readers because of low educational standards.
2. _____Students must aim for perfectionism in reading.
3. _____The way one reads is a habit.
4. _____Reading whole thoughts increases comprehension.
5. _____Tripling one's reading speed may result in a decrease in comprehension.

Now that you have had some practice in using larger spanning movements, you can take the different types of reading exercises which follow. They are designed to help you improve both reading speed and comprehension. Before and after each exercise you will find a place to mark the time you begin and end and the reading time (the difference between the beginning and ending time). After each selection there is a table which will help you find your approximate reading speed. Comprehension tests are included for some of the exercises.

The first exercise is a "warm-up." It is short, but each paragraph contains a number of ideas.

Exercise 1   **(170 words)**

Beginning Time: Hr: ___ Min: ___ Sec: ___

Some students use a study method which may be termed "Situation Response," "Idea Response," or "Concept Response." This method employs the subheading, key sentence, or key word of each paragraph as a clue to recalling all the material related to the idea. This system seems to work best for subjects such as English, Psychology, Health Education, and Speech.

In other subjects (History, Biology, Geology) that require the memorization of specific materials such as dates, groups of words, or vocabulary, it is very helpful to use word lists on 3 x 5 cards or flash cards that can be carried in purse or pocket.

Another method which might be labeled "Rewriting Class Material" seems to be effective for many students, especially if the instructor has jumped around over the subject matter or has talked in circles while lecturing. This rewriting of class notes helps in retaining the material longer. It also enables the student to collect and reorganize his notes in a logical order. New associations are more readily seen by using this method.

Ending Time: Hr: ___ Min: ___ Sec: ___
Reading Time: Min: ___ Sec: ___

Min.	Sec.	Words Per Min.
	20	510
	30	340
	40	265
	50	220
1	–	170
1	10	145
1	20	130

You may have found the reading test you have just taken more difficult than the first one. This is because the material contains a greater concentration of ideas, and there are more points to be remembered.

The next exercise is an excerpt from John Steinbeck's short story, *The Red Pony*.[2] Compare your reading time for this test with the time for the preceding one.

Exercise 2   **(555 words)**

Beginning Time: Hr: ___ Min: ___ Sec: ___

A red pony colt was looking at him out of the stall. Its tense ears were forward and a light of disobedience was in its eyes. Its coat was rough and thick as an airedale's fur and its mane was long and tangled. Jody's throat collapsed in on itself and cut his breath short.

"He needs a good currying," his father said, "and if I ever hear of you not feeding him or leaving his stall dirty, I'll sell him off in a minute."

Jody couldn't bear to look at the pony's eyes any more. He gazed down at his hands for a moment, and he asked very shyly, "Mine?" No one answered him. He put his hand out toward the pony. Its grey nose came close, sniffing loudly, and then the lips drew back and the strong teeth closed on Jody's fingers. The pony shook its head up and down and seemed to laugh with amusement. Jody regarded his bruised fingers. "Well," he said with pride—"Well, I guess he can bite all right." The two men laughed, somewhat in relief. Carl Tiflin went out of the barn and walked up a side-hill to be by himself, for he was embarrassed, but Billy Buck stayed. It was easier to talk to Billy Buck. Jody asked again—"Mine?"

Billy became professional in tone. "Sure! That is, if you look out for him

and break him right. I'll show you how. He's just a colt. You can't ride him for some time."

Jody put out his bruised hand again, and this time the red pony let his nose be rubbed. "I ought to have a carrot," Jody said. "Where'd we get him, Billy?"

"Bought him at a sheriff's auction," Billy explained. "A show went broke in Salinas and had debts. The sheriff was selling off their stuff."

The pony stretched out his nose and shook the forelock from his wild eyes. Jody stroked the nose a little. He said softly, "There isn't a—saddle?"

Billy Buck laughed. "I'd forgot. Come along."

In the harness room he lifted down a little saddle of red morocco leather. "It's just a show saddle," Billy Buck said disparagingly. "It isn't practical for the brush, but it was cheap at the sale."

Jody couldn't trust himself to look at the saddle either, and he couldn't speak at all. He brushed the shining red leather with his fingertips, and after a long time he said, "It'll look pretty on him though." He thought of the grandest and prettiest things he knew. "If he hasn't a name already, I think I'll call him Gabilan Mountains," he said.

Billy Buck knew how he felt. "It's a pretty long name. Why don't you just call him Gabilan? That means hawk. That would be a fine name for him." Billy felt glad. "If you will collect tail hair, I might be able to make a hair rope for you sometime. You could use it for a hackamore."

Jody wanted to go back to the box stall. "Could I lead him to school, do you think— to show the kids?"

But Billy shook his head. "He's not even halter-broke yet. We had a time getting him here. Had to almost drag him. You better be starting for school though."

"I'll bring the kids to see him here this afternoon," Jody said.

Ending Time: Hr: ___ Min: ___ Sec: ___
Reading Time: Min: ___ Sec: ___

Min.	Sec.	Words Per Min.
1	—	555
1	10	475
1	20	415
1	30	370
1	40	335
1	50	305
2	—	280
2	10	255
2	20	235
2	30	225

In contrast to the fiction excerpt you have just read, the next two exercises (Exercise 3 and Exercise 4) will be selections from a technical book on psychology, *Theories of Learning,* by Ernest R. Hilgard.[3] Since you know the material will be difficult, you should be prepared to read more slowly and to absorb more information. This will help you in answering the questions, which will also be rather difficult.

A different approach has been used in the comprehension tests. The lines of the reading tests have been numbered, and a line reference is given for each question; you must find the answers.

Compare your reading time and speed for the fiction exercise and the technical ones which follow.

Exercise 3 (740 words)

Beginning Time: Hr: ___ Min: ___ Sec: ___

1   Learning theorists commonly select one kind of learning problem or situation
2   as typical and then proceed to develop a theory appropriate to this reference
3   situation. Having constructed a set of principles in this way, they attempt to
4   show by a logical process that other kinds of learning are really at base like the
5   typical one, and hence explicable in the same terms. Recognizing this tendency,
6   Tolman selected for review three kinds of learning experiments, with their three
7   corresponding doctrines. These were conditioned-reflex learning (Pavlov), trial-
8   and-error learning (Thorndike), and inventive learning (Köhler). He then gave a
9   sign-gestalt interpretation of each of the three kinds of learning as alternative
10   to the usual theory associated with each. He found it useful to preserve the
11   typical experiments, which represent a kind of hierarchy from stupidity to in-
12   telligence. The laws applicable to the more stupid situations have to be
13   supplemented by additional laws for higher forms of learning.
14   In the 1932 version there are three groups of laws: capacity laws, laws
15   relative to the nature of the material, and laws relative to the manner of
16   presentation.
17   1. *Capacity laws.* Only organisms can learn. It is evident, therefore,
18   that what the organism can learn must depend on what kind of an organism it is.
19   That is the reason for capacity laws.
20   The list of capacity laws is as follows: °
21   a. Formal means-end-capacities
22   b. Discriminating and manipulating capacities
23   c. Retentivity
24   d. Means-end-capacities needed for alternative routes, detours, etc.

° E. C. Tolman, *Purposive Behavior in Animals and Men,* New York, D. Appleton-Century (Reprinted, University of California Press, 1949), pp. 385–389.

25   e. Ideational capacities
26   f. Creative instability
27   In order to learn conditioned reflexes, the learner must have the necessary
28   capacities to form and act in accordance with "sign-gestalt-expectations."   That
29   is, the conditioned stimulus serves as a sign that the unconditioned stimulus is
30   about to appear and the conditioned behavior is appropriate to the sign.   This
31   capacity is named a "means-end-capacity."   In his later writings Tolman has
32   dropped a number of the hyphenated terms which make his book clear, entertaining,
33   but also somewhat forbidding.   In the list of laws which we have given above, his
34   terms have been freely paraphrased to make for easier reading, although there may
35   be some loss involved.   In addition to the general capacity for sign learning,
36   conditioning requires special capacities for discriminating and manipulating
37   features of the environment.   Finally retentivity is implied, if the results of
38   earlier conditioning trials are to influence later ones.   Only capacity laws a, b
39   and c apply to conditioning.
40   The capacities needed for trial-and-error learning are the same as those re-
41   quired for conditioning, except that additional means-end-capacities are needed
42   because more alternatives are open to the learner.   The field relationships of
43   alternate routes, detours, final common paths, are involved.   Additional capaci-
44   ties of ideational sort, permitting comparison of alternatives (a mental "running-
45   back-and-forth") are probably helpful in trial-and-error learning.
46   Inventive learning requires all the capacities of the other varieties of
47   learning plus *creative instability*.   This is a capacity to break out into new
48   lines of activity which have never occurred to the learner before.
49   The need for capacity laws seems evident enough, once they are proposed,
50   though they have been neglected in most learning theories.   Even Thorndike,
51   strongly identified with the study of individual differences, neglects capacity
52   laws in his learning theory.   Such a statement as "Any response of which the or-
53   ganism is capable can become attached to any stimulus to which it is sensitive" †
54   implies only sensitivity capacity and response capacity, and neglects any
55   capacity to establish relations between them.   It would be grossly unfair to say
56   that Thorndike did not recognize differences in learning ability, but it is true
57   that he slighted the different kinds of capacities needed for different kinds of
58   learning, because all learning was merely the forming of bonds.   Hull, who also
59   in one of his earlier research interests contributed to the psychology of indi-
60   vidual differences,‡ only late in his career began to consider individuality as
61   something to enter into his learning theory.§

† E. L. Thorndike, *The Psychology of Learning* (*Educational Psychology, II*), New York, Teachers College, page 15.

‡ C. L. Hull, *Aptitude Testing*, Yonkers-on-Hudson, New York, World Book.

§ C. L. Hull, "The Place of Innate Individual and Species Differences in a Natural-Science Theory of Behavior," *Psychological Review*, 1945, **52**, 55–60.

Ending Time: Hr: —— Min: —— Sec: ——
Reading Time: Min: —— Sec: ——

Min.	Sec.	Words Per Min.
1	—	740
1	30	495
2	—	370
2	30	315
3	—	245
3	30	210
4	—	185
4	30	165

Comprehension Test for Exercise 3

LINES

1–3	(1)	How are learning theories commonly developed?
7–8	(2)	What are the three learning experiments reviewed by Tolman?
7–8	(3)	Who originated each experiment?
9	(4)	What is a "sign-gestalt" interpretation?
9–10	(5)	Why did Tolman give a sign-gestalt interpretation to each of the three kinds of learning?
14–16	(6)	Name the three groups of learning laws.
17–19	(7)	What is the reason for capacity laws?
20–26	(8)	Name the six capacity laws.
*	(9)	Who originated them?
*	(10)	In what book were the capacity laws originally published?
27–31	(11)	What is a "means-end-capacity"?
38–39	(12)	Which of the capacity laws apply to conditioning?
40–45	(13)	What are the capacities need for trial-and-error learning?
40–42	(14)	Are the capacities required for trial-and-error learning different from those needed for conditioning?
47	(15)	What particular capacity is required in inventive learning?
47–48	(16)	What is "creative instability"?
27–48	(17)	Explain each of the capacity laws in your own words.
50–52	(18)	Does Thorndike emphasize capacity laws in his learning theory?
58	(19)	What is Thorndike's basic belief about learning?
58–61	(20)	What was Hull's attitude toward the importance of individuality in learning?

You may have found it necessary to reread the selection in order to answer the questions. In doing so, did you find that you got much more from the material than when you had no questions to answer? You're reading now for association of ideas rather than for speed. If you had known what to look for while you were reading, you probably would have read differently. Even though it takes more time, reading with a purpose pays dividends.

* See footnote on page 61.

You probably encountered at least one question which could not be answered by reading the material. This is meant to remind you that in reading matter of this type you will often have to use the index as well as other books and dictionaries to find the meanings of technical words, phrases, and concepts. You should also be aware of the footnotes, which contain valuable and helpful information.

As you read the second half of this selection, try to visualize the questions that will be asked. You will not be reading as fast as when trying to maintain speed or as slowly as when trying to answer specific questions, but you will get more for the time spent in reading.

Exercise 4 (580 words)

Beginning Time: Hr: ___ Min: ___ Sec: ___

1   2. *Laws relating to the nature of the material.* In Tolman's discussion
2   of these topics, he calls attention to certain "gestalt-inducing-conditions" and
3   suggests that they are of the sorts emphasized in gestalt studies of perception.
4   The list follows: *
5   a. Togetherness
6   b. Fusibility
7   c. Other gestalt-like laws
8   d. Interrelations among the spatial, temporal and other characters
9   of the alternatives
10   e. Characters in the material favoring new closures and expansions
11   of the field
12   In relation to conditioned-reflex learning, these laws suggest that there
13 must be a "togetherness" of essential signs and their means-end-relationship to
14 the thing signified. Tolman states that this is about what Thorndike has called
15 "belongingness." Tolman adds a somewhat similar law of fusibility of sign, sig-
16 nificate, and signified means-end-relationship by which he means a certain
17 naturalness about the situation which makes it easier to form a gestalt of the
18 whole. He provides in a third law for the possibility of new discoveries. He
19 adds one law (d) for trial-and-error learning and one for inventive learning (e),
20 to suggest that some arrangements must be easier than others. He points to
21 Kohler's observation that the ape could learn to use the stick more easily to
22 rake in the food if the stick and food were perceived together.
23   These laws show great catholicity, but there is no ordering principle
24 among them. "Spatial, temporal, and other" can scarcely be said to arrange
25 things dimensionally. They do make a definite bow to the important fact that
26 perceptual principles must be understood if the relative ease or difficulty of
27 problematic situations is to be made comprehensible.
28   3. *Laws relative to the manner of presentation.* These are the laws in-
29 herited largely from association psychology, the ones for which abundant evidence
30 can be found recorded in McGeoch and Irion's book (1952). The list is as follows: †
31   a. Frequency, recency
32   b. Revival after extinction, primacy, distributed repetition, etc.
33   c. Motivation

* Tolman, pages 378–385.
† Tolman, pages 385–389.

34   d. Not "effect" but "emphasis"
35   e. Temporal orders and sequences in the presentation of alternatives
36   f. Temporal relations between the presentation of certain of the already
37   given alternatives and the true solution
38   Of these, the first four belong to conditioned-reflex learning, and all
39 six to inventive learning.
40   The principles of frequency and recency are accepted in the following form:
41 "The more frequently and more recently the actual sequence of sign, means-end-
42 relation and significate have been presented, the stronger, other things being
43 equal, this resulting sign-gestalt will tend to be." ‡ That is, only in a
44 situation favorable to sign-gestalt formation will frequency be effective. The
45 other laws provide opportunity again to raise the question of the law of effect,
46 and to make some observations descriptive of favorable conditions in trial-and-
47 error and multiple choice experiments.
48   As a set, the laws are rather disappointing. They serve as a useful re-
49 minder of the main tenets of the point of view and of its criticisms of prevailing
50 doctrines. They leave much to be asked for on the positive side in their lack of
51 sufficient precision of statement so that they can be called true or false.
52   Leaving the laws in this form makes everything a matter of correlations
53 between situation and behavior and does not get at the formal problem of
54 rigorous definition and measurement of intervening variables. This lack has not
55 yet been made up, in spite of later reworkings of the list of laws.

Ending Time: Hr: ___ Min: ___ Sec: ___
Reading Time: Min: ___ Sec: ___

Min.	Sec.	Words Per Min.
1	—	580
1	20	435
1	40	350
2	—	290
2	20	250
2	40	215
3	—	195
3	20	175
3	40	160
4	—	145

Comprehension Test for Exercise 4

LINES
4–11   (1) What are the five conditions which Tolman calls "gestalt-inducing"?
12–22   (2) Explain in your own words each of the laws relating to the nature of the
        material.
23   (3) Explain "catholicity."
23–24   (4) How would you define an "ordering principle"?
25–27   (5) What is the important fact emphasized by these laws?

‡ Tolman, page 386.

Comprehension Test for Exercise 4 *(Continued)*

LINES

28–29   (6) The laws relative to the manner of presentation are derived from what branch of psychology?

39–47   (7) Explain each of these laws in your own words. What authors are named
30   whose work might help you learn about these laws?

38–39   (8) To what categories of learning do these laws belong?

40–44   (9) In what kind of situation will the principles of frequency and recency be effective?

48–56   (10) What are the positive and negative aspects of these laws?

The next two reading exercises (Exercise 5 and Exercise 6) are taken from *Vitalized Chemistry,* by Russell T. Des Jardins.[4] Your reading rate will be slowed down even more than it was for the psychological material. This is because of the mathematics involved in the formulas and problems. But remember that reading by thought units will help you increase your speed even with difficult scientific material. Read through the first test using large spanning movements; check to see if your rate has improved after doing the same thing with the second exercise.

Exercise 5   **(640 words)**

Beginning Time: Hr: ___ Min: ___ Sec: ___

Percentage Composition from Formula. The formula of a compound, being an exact representation of the make-up of the molecule, permits us to calculate the per cent of the weight of a compound which is due to any particular part of the compound. For example, we might wish to know what part of the weight of water is due to hydrogen—we would then know how much hydrogen can be obtained by decomposing say, one kilogram of water. We might also wish to know what per cent of the weight of crystallized copper sulfate is water of crystallization—we could then tell how much water we were buying in a pound of copper sulfate crys-

tals. Similarly, in mining operations, it is important to know just what yield of pure metal can be expected from a given ore. In all these problems, the knowledge of the formula of the compound makes the solution relatively simple.

TYPE PROBLEM

Determine the percentage composition of mercuric chloride ($HgCl_2$).

Method: By means of the formula and atomic weights, determine what per cent of the molecular weight is due to each element in the compound.

SOLUTION

At. Wt. of Hg. = 200; At. Wt. of Cl = 35.5

M.W. of $HgCl_2$ = 200 + 2 (35.5) = 271

$$\%Hg: \frac{\text{Wt. due to Hg}}{\text{Mol. Wt.}} = \frac{200}{271}$$

$$= 0.738, \quad \text{or} \quad 73.8\%$$

$$\%Cl: \frac{\text{Wt. due to } Cl_2}{\text{Mol. Wt.}} = \frac{71}{271}$$

$$= 0.262, \quad \text{or} \quad \frac{26.2\%}{100.0\%}$$

Note. There are two atoms of chlorine in the molecule; therefore there are 71 units of weight due to chlorine.

Formula from Percentage Composition. A more common problem than that just considered is its exact opposite: *Given the percentage composition of a compound, determine its true formula.* This problem often arises when new substances are synthesized in the laboratory, or when unknown substances have to be identified. It is particularly frequent in the field of organic chemistry, where thousands of different compounds can be formed from the same few elements.

If the molecular weight of the unknown compound has been determined (methods of determining molecular weight are described on page 100), the exact formula of the compound can be calculated from its composition. If the molecular weight is *not* known, the best that can be done is to obtain the "simplest" possible formula, which is not necessarily the true formula. The method of solving the problem depends on whether or not the molecular weight is known.

Case 1. Molecular Weight Is Known. This is the easier of the two cases. By applying the known percentage composition to the known molecular weight, the part of the weight contributed by each element is found. This partial weight is then divided by the weight of a single atom (the atomic weight of the element) to determine how many atoms of that element must be present in the molecule.

TYPE PROBLEM

Determine the formula of a substance whose molecular weight is 230, and which is composed of 65.2% arsenic and 34.8% oxygen.

SOLUTION

Weight due to arsenic = $65.2\% \times 230 = 150$
Weight due to oxygen = $34.8\% \times 230 = 80$
——
(Total: 230)

At. Wt. of As = 75; 150/75 = 2 atoms of As
At. Wt. of O = 16; 80/16 = 5 atoms of O

Formula is, therefore, As_2O_5

Note. The procedure is that of the percentage composition problem worked backwards.

Case 2. Molecular Weight Is Not Known. The formula of ethylene is C_2H_4; that of propylene is C_3H_6. It is apparent that these two compounds have the same percentage composition (try it and see). If, therefore, we were given only the percentage composition, and not the molecular weight, there would be no way of determining whether the formula were C_2H_4, C_3H_6, or $C_{100}H_{200}$. However, we could discover that, whatever the actual formula is, it contains 2 atoms of hydrogen for every atom of carbon. Let us see how this is done.

Ending Time: Hr: ___ Min: ___ Sec: ___
Reading Time: Min: ___ Sec: ___

Min.	Sec.	Words Per Min.
1	—	640
1	20	480
1	40	385
2	—	320
2	20	275
2	40	240
3	—	215
3	40	175
4	—	160

Exercise 6 **(690 words)**

Beginning Time: Hr: ___ Min: ___ Sec: ___

CALCIUM AND ITS COMPOUNDS

Occurrence. Calcium, like sodium and potassium occurs only in compounds in nature, because of its great activity. Unlike the alkali metals, calcium has two electrons in its valence shell and hence has a valence of +2.

Calcium compounds are very common in the earth's crust. The commonest calcium compound is the *carbonate.* Other important natural compounds include: *gypsum* ($CaSO_4 \cdot 2H_2O$), *phosphorite*

$(Ca_3(PO_4)_2)$, *apatite* $(3Ca_3(PO_4)_2\cdot CaF_2)$, and *dolomite* $(CaCO_3\cdot MgCO_3)$. Calcium is present in the bones as *tricalcium phosphate*, the calcium content of the body being about 1.5 per cent.

Preparation. The usual method for the preparation of calcium is by the electrolysis of fused calcium chloride. The metal is liberated in the molten state and floats to the surface of the bath from which it is cooled and slowly lifted as an irregular stick of metallic calcium.

Properties. Calcium is a silvery-white metal, harder than silver and slightly lighter than aluminum. It reacts slowly with cold water to release hydrogen and form calcium hydroxide:

$$Ca + 2H\,O \rightarrow Ca(OH)_2 + H\uparrow$$

Uses. Calcium has found increasing use as a deoxidizer in ferrous metallurgy and as an alloy component with non-ferrous metals. It has been employed in the reduction of metals difficult to reduce, such as chromium, thorium, uranium, and zirconium. During the war, an important calcium use was to make the hydride (CaH_2), which is a convenient and portable source of hydrogen.

Calcium Carbonate. Deposits of impure forms of calcium carbonate are found in many countries. These have been formed during past geologic ages from the shells of sea animals, converted under pressure to *limestone, chalk,* and the crystalline form *marble. Calcite* and *aragonite* are pure forms of the compound which occur naturally.

Limestone Caves. Calcium carbonite is relatively insoluble in water, but when water containing carbon dioxide comes in contact with calcium carbonate soluble calcium bicarbonate is formed. Caves are formed in limestone regions as a result of this reaction.

$$CaCO_3 + H_2O + CO_2 \rightarrow Ca(HCO_3)_2$$

Caves such as the *Luray Caverns* of Virginia, the *Mammoth Cave* of Kentucky and the *Carlsbad Cavern* of New Mexico have been formed by this type of action.

When water saturated with calcium bicarbonate seeps through the roof of such caverns, some of the water evaporates, causing the reversal of the above reaction:

$$Ca(HCO_3)_2 \rightarrow CaCO_3 + H_2O + CO_2\uparrow$$

This accounts for the slow formation of stalactites and stalagmites in these caves. *Stalactites* are limestone masses hanging from the roof of a cave, while *stalagmites* are limestone masses deposited on the floor of the cave.

Properties of Calcium Carbonate. Calcium carbonate is a white solid. When pure and crystallized, as in calcite, it is transparent. It is insoluble in water but soluble in water containing carbon dioxide. It reacts with acids to form carbon dioxide and a salt of the acid:

$$CaCO_3 + H_2SO_4 \rightarrow CaSO_4 + H_2O + CO_2\uparrow$$

$$CaCO_3 + 2HCl \rightarrow CaCl_2 + H_2O + CO_2\uparrow$$

When heated, calcium carbonate yields calcium oxide and carbon dioxide.

USES

1. *As a building material,* forms of calcium carbonate such as limestone, travertine and marble are frequently used. Not only do these materials have excellent structural strength but they add greatly to the beauty of many buildings. Marble is familiar as an ornamental stone. Fossillized limestone, in which the skeletons of sea animals are plainly visible, is used to ornament the walls of the Canadian House of Parliament in Ottawa.

2. Limestone is also used for the manufacture of calcium oxide (*quicklime*), which has many important industrial uses.

3. The essential materials used in the manufacture of calcium oxide (*quicklime*),

which has many important industrial uses.

4. Ground limestone is sometimes applied to the soil to *counteract the acidity of soils.*

5. It is also an important raw material *in the manufacture of glass* and ceramic substances.

6. Calcium carbonate is used *as a flux in the smelting of iron ore.*

7. Limestone, as you will recall, is also one of the basic materials used *in the Solvay Process* for the manufacture of sodium carbonate.

Ending Time: Hr: —— Min: —— Sec: ——
Reading Time: Min: —— Sec: ——

Min.	Sec.	Words Per Min.
1	—	690
1	20	515
1	40	415
2	—	345
2	20	295
2	40	260
3	—	230
3	20	205
3	40	185
4	—	175

No comprehension tests have been prepared for these last two reading exercises. Instead, space is being provided below for you to make your own tests. This is an opportunity for you to see how well you can pick out the important points in difficult reading matter.

Comprehension Test for Exercise 5

Comprehension Test for Exercise 6

Reading Scores Achieved by a Sample Group

The reading exercises and comprehension tests in this chapter were given to a group of 386 college freshmen. It was not intended that this group should be representative of college freshmen; the author merely wished to see how a sample of college students read mimeographed material when they felt they were not being tested for grading purposes. One interesting result of this observation was that the average reading speed of this group was found to be about 250 words per minute. Several authorities have tested college students and have found that under test conditions with certain types of material they read about 300 words per minute. If many freshmen are reading at the rate of 250 rather than 300 words per minute, there is a great need for improvement.

This test group read Exercise 1 in an average time of 45 seconds. There was considerable variation in the way these people were able to answer the questions that followed. The ones who were able to answer only one question correctly had a median reading time of 60 seconds or about 170 words per minute. Those who were able to get two right read at the rate of 188 words per minute, with a median rate of 54 seconds. The students who were able to answer three questions right read the exercise in 44 seconds, and those who got four right read it in 40 seconds. The people who answered all the questions correctly read the exercise at the rate of 286 words per minute and finished it on the average in 37 seconds. From this and other studies, it becomes evident that the faster readers are also those who achieve better comprehension.

The reading time for Exercise 2 for the test group of students ranged from 75 seconds to 190 seconds. The median time was 115 seconds.

Both Exercise 3 and 4 appeared to be quite difficult for the sample group. The range of reading time for Exercise 3 was from 80 seconds to 290 seconds; the number of correct answers ranged from 0 to 12. The median for correct answers was 4, and the median reading time was 170 seconds. For Exercise 4, the range of reading time was from 65 seconds to 260 seconds, with a median of 160 seconds. However, the rate of comprehension was quite low at this rate of speed. The median of comprehension was only one right out of the ten questions. No one was able to answer more than 7 correctly.

These scores definitely indicate that material of this level of difficulty requires greater concentration and a slowing down in the reading rate in order that the ideas being presented may be absorbed. If you try to push yourself through text material of this type at the same reading speed you use for easier material, you are less likely to become really involved with the subject matter. This will hamper you in attaining the necessary proficiency for answering test questions and making a satisfactory course grade. In order to read and comprehend with a fair degree of understanding and ease, the individual student must use the knowledge he has gained from experience about his requirements and limitations.

Although women are generally more rapid readers than men, in certain technical and mathematical areas men seem to be able to comprehend better and read faster. This is pointed out merely to show that individuals should be cognizant of all factors related to their ability and background that may be involved in understanding what they read. In Exercises 5 and 6, the male and female scores were separated to see if this variation occurred in the group being tested; the results show that the women were reading this technical material more slowly than the men.

On Exercise 5, the students in the test group had a range of reading time from 95 seconds to 300 seconds; the median for women was 180 seconds and for men, 165. For Exercise 6, the range of time was from 115 seconds to 300 seconds. The medians were 205 seconds for the women and 175 seconds for the men.

The following chart will help you compare the · number of words you read per minute for each exercise with the rate achieved by the sample group of college students. The figures are given in rounded numbers.

Words Per Minute

	Slowest	Median	Fastest
Exercise 1	125	255	680
Exercise 2	175	290	445
Exercise 3	155	265	555
Exercise 4	135	215	535
Exercise 5			
Male	145	230	405
Female	130	215	405
Exercise 6			
Male	165	235	435
Female	140	210	360

The student should realize that these reading exercises are not intended to be a substitute for standarized reading tests. However, they may make him aware of his degree of reading efficiency so that he can take the needed steps toward improvement. When standardized tests are available, the student would do well to take them.

References

1. Lyle Tussing, "Perceptual Fluctuations of Illusions as a Possible Physical Fatigue Index," *Journal of Experimental Psychology*, 1941, **29**, 185–188.
2. From *The Red Pony*, by John Steinbeck. Copyright 1937 by John Steinbeck. Reprinted by permission of The Viking Press.
3. Ernest R. Hilgard, *Theories of Learning*, New York, Appleton-Century-Crofts, copyright 1956, pp. 202–206; 252–254.
4. Russell T. Des Jardins, *Vitalized Chemistry*, New York, College Entrance Book Co., 1957, pp. 90–93; 216–218.

Key to True-False Quiz

(1) F   (2) F   (3) T   (4) T   (5) F

6

FINDING MATERIAL

THE LIBRARY

College is a series of problems. The student who can use books properly is able to solve many of these problems. It is hoped this chapter will help the student improve his ability to find and utilize the information stored in books.

The term paper is an example of a problem encountered in college. One reason instructors assign a term paper is to familiarize the student with library facilities. This assignment re-

quires the student to gather large amounts of information about one subject.

The library may be compared to an enormous book in which the classification system is similar to chapters and each book represents a page. Just as a book is not assembled haphazardly, so is a library put together in a completely orderly way. Just as an informative book will have both a table of contents and a detailed index to guide the reader in his search for specific information, so will an efficient library have a classification plan and guides to its contents. There are three main guides to the information in the library:

I. The card catalogue
II. Indexes to periodicals
III. General reference books

I. The Library Card Catalogue

Most libraries use call numbers on their cards based on either the Library of Congress Classification or the Dewey Decimal System. In most cases only large universities use the Library of Congress method which is based on the alphabet. It is more flexible than the Dewey Decimal System, making it convenient to use with a very large number of books. However, many libraries use this system for cross-reference, mainly for the use of the librarian. The Dewey Decimal System, which is based on numbers, is the one most widely used in public libraries and colleges. It is arranged as follows:

> 000 General Works
> 100 Philosophy
> 200 Religion
> 300 Sociology
> 400 Philology
> 500 Natural Science
> 600 Useful Arts
> 700 Fine Arts
> 800 Literature
> 900 History

Each of these main divisions is divided again into ten smaller divisions, and each one of these again into ten subdivisions. This subdividing can go on indefinitely through the use of decimals.

Most libraries usually have posted near the entrance an outline of the classification system; also, the librarian is always willing to give explanations and answer any questions to which you have not been able to find answers.

The card catalogue usually has three cards (and often more) for every book in the library: one card giving the author first, one card giving the title first, and one card giving the subject first. All three cards are basically the same otherwise. Not all libraries are able to use this three-card system, but there will always be a card for every book filed under the author's name. An "author" card generally contains the following information:

1. Call number—indicates in what part of the library and on what shelf the book may be found
2. Name of author or authors (last name first)

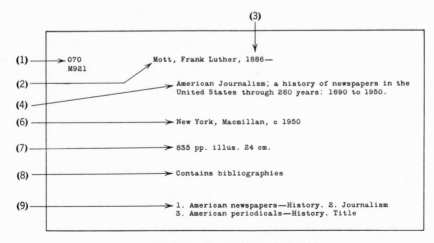

A SAMPLE LIBRARY CATALOGUE CARD

3. Author's date of birth (and death, if no longer living)
4. Book title
5. Edition number, if not first edition
6. Place of publication, name of publisher, and date of publication
7. Number of pages in book, illustrations (if any), and height of book in centimeters
8. Bibliography (if book has one)
9. Indication that book also has subject and title cards in the catalogue

II. Indexes to Periodicals

Quite often, a term paper needs to be rounded out with up-to-date information. Because books have to be prepared over a period of time, they may not always contain the latest information. A newspaper or magazine article may supply just the recent information necessary.

The periodical indexes are volumes which classify articles in periodicals (newspapers and magazines) just as the card catalogue does with books: an article is listed under author, subject, and sometimes under title. These indexes are compiled as quickly as possible after the periodicals appear.

Periodical indexes are compiled both for general information and for specific fields. Some of the more widely used indexes are listed below:

General Indexes

Readers' Guide to Periodical Literature. This index has covered widely read magazines since 1906 and has the subject and author indexing with cross references. It is probably the most extensively used magazine index today.

International Index to Periodicals. This is an author and subject index to material published since 1907. It covers many learned and professional journals in the humanities and social sciences not included in the *Readers' Guide.* Also, it lists foreign as well as American periodicals.

Poole's Index to Periodical Literature. This is an index to British and American magazines published from 1802 to 1906, and it is valuable for finding articles published before 1907. It is a subject index only.

New York Times Index. This index lists material printed since 1913 in the *New York Times,* one of the most objective and comprehensive newspapers in the world. It contains subject listings.

Special Indexes

Art Index. 1929–
Agricultural Index. 1916–
Dramatic Index. 1909–
Education Index. 1929–
Engineering Index. 1884–
Industrial Arts Index. 1913–
Music Index. 1949–
Psychological Index. 1894–1936
Public Affairs Information Service. 1915–
Technical Book Review Index. 1917–1929; 1935–

Indexes for Abstracts

Magazines which contain summaries of books and articles written in specialized fields are called abstracts. These are valuable sources of information for researchers in specific areas. Abstracts are titled according to the subject—for example, *Biological Abstracts, Chemical Abstracts, Abstracts of English Literature,* and *Psychological Abstracts.* Abstracts are compiled into yearly volumes; each volume has an index listing subjects and authors.

III. General Reference Books

The reference library consists of a large number of works such as encyclopedias, dictionaries, and atlases. A good way to begin research on any subject is to consult a reference book, because it will give a basic, overall view of the topic. Usually a good bibliography is included with each article; this can be a guide to further research.

Encyclopedias. Encyclopedias range from one-volume works (illustrations eliminated by necessity) to sets of twenty-four and thirty volumes. These sets are continually being revised and have annual supplements. Foreign encyclopedias are often excellently illustrated and are especially valuable on matters pertaining to the culture of the country represented. Encyclopedias are divided into those which furnish general views of a subject and those which deal with special subjects.

General Encyclopedias
Collier's Encyclopedia. 20 vols.
Columbia Encyclopedia.
Encyclopedia Americana. 30 vols.
Encyclopedia Britannica. 24 vols.
Lincoln Library of Essential Information.
New International Encyclopaedia. 27 vols.

Special Encyclopedias
Encyclopedia of Religion and Ethics. 13 vols.
Encyclopedia of the Social Sciences. 15 vols.
Harper's Encyclopedia of Art. 2 vols.
Jones, Franklin D. *Engineering Encyclopedia.* 2 vols.
Monroe, Walter S. *Encyclopedia of Educational Research.*
Theimer, Walter. *Encyclopedia of Modern World Politics.*
Thompson, Oscar. *International Encyclopedia of Music and Musicians.*
Van Nostrand's Scientific Encyclopedia.

Yearbooks
These books deal with current events and statistics about government, trade, etc. They also give biographical facts about important people.

Britannica Book of the Year. 1938–
Information Please Almanac. 1947–
New International Yearbook. 1907–
World Almanac and Book of Facts. 1868–

Dictionaries. Dictionaries are basic tools which can help the student improve his powers of understanding and communication through the proper use of language. Unabridged dictionaries contain technical terms and other information not usually found in desk dictionaries. They are very large and costly and are more suitable for library than private use.

A good desk dictionary contains definitions of words used in general speech and non-technical reading matter. When technical words are used so often they come into general usage, they appear in the desk dictionary. This type of dictionary also contains information about the origin and development of words and records changes in usage.

The student needs a personal dictionary that is not too expensive, portable, accurate, and as complete as possible. As a general rule, the cheap, paperbacked, condensed dictionary is not suitable for college work. Usually college English teachers recommend to their students one or two dictionaries which they consider satisfactory. These dictionaries are among the ones most often recommended:

Macmillan's Modern Dictionary.
New College Standard Dictionary.
The American College Dictionary.
Thorndike-Barnhart Comprehensive Desk Dictionary.
Webster's New Collegiate Dictionary.
Webster's New World Dictionary of the American Language.

The dictionary's main purpose is to define words; however, it can also help to improve spelling and pronunciation. The college student should train himself to use the keys to pronunciàtion and to understand the special labels given to words, such as obsolete, colloquial, British, slang, etc. The introductory material in a dictionary will provide the information needed to understand and properly use this valuable reference work.

As with encyclopedias, dictionaries may deal with general or specialized matter. There are dictionaries of abbreviations and scientific terms, and others in the fields of law, medicine, education, etc. Only a few can be listed here.

General Dictionaries (Unabridged)

New Century Dictionary of the English Language. 2 vols.
New Standard Dictionary of the English Language.
Oxford English Dictionary. 13 vols.
Webster's New International Dictionary of the English Language.

Special Dictionaries

Bartlett, John. *Familiar Quotations.*
Black's Law Dictionary.
Evans, Bergen and Cornelia. *A Dictionary of Contemporary American Usage.*
Fowler, H. W. *A Dictionary of Modern English Usage.*
Mencken, H. W. *A New Dictionary of Quotations on Historical Principles.*

Roget, P. M. *Thesaurus of English Words and Phrases.*
Webster's Dictionary of Synonyms.

Gazeteers and atlases. Gazeteers list names of places alphabetically with some geographical information about each place. Atlases are books usually made up entirely of maps. Sometimes both kinds of material are included in one book. Atlases can also be made up entirely of pictures pertaining to one subject, such as architectural forms or human anatomical components. A few names of this type of reference work are given here:

Atlas of American History.
Columbia Lippincott Gazeteer of the World.
Encyclopaedia Britannica World Atlas. Revised annually.
Webster's Geographical Dictionary.

Test Yourself on Chapter 6

1. Newspaper articles are classified in _____ indexes.

2. The library card catalogue usually has at least three types of cards for each book: (1) _____ (2) _____ (3) _____.

3. Why is consulting an encyclopedia or dictionary a good way to begin research on any subject? _____.

4. The three main guides to information on the library are: (1) _____ (2) _____ (3) _____.

5. The classification system most widely used in college libraries is _____.

Know Your Library

As soon as possible, schedule at least an hour for getting acquainted with your school library. Besides the information available in books and periodicals, the library offers other valuable facilities. Also there are certain rules which the student must follow. As you are browsing through the library, look for the answers to these questions:

1. Is the library open on Saturdays? _____ Sundays? _____ What are the hours during the week? _____ On weekends? _____

2. For how long may library books be borrowed? _____ What is the fine for overdue books? _____

3. What is the time limit for using books "on reserve"? _____ What is the fine for overdue reserve books? _____ May reserve books ever be taken out of the library? _____ When? _____

4. Find out if your library provides these facilities, and write down the locations and any special rules:
Record collections and listening rooms _____

Pictures and records which may be borrowed _____

Study rooms _____
Typing rooms _____
Exhibits (art, science, etc.) _____

Make a list of any other features of your school library that are not mentioned here.

7

ORGANIZING MATERIAL AND TAKING NOTES

OUTLINING

An outline is one of the most important tools for successful writing and study. The main purpose of outlining is to organize ideas logically and effectively. An outline can be thought of as a map to guide you to an exact destination, a blueprint which you can follow or change if need be, or a framework around which you fit material to build your structure. Outlining can be of great value to you in two ways—writing papers and taking notes.

The two kinds of outlines most often used are the topic outline and the sentence outline. In the topic outline, brief phrases or single words are used. The sentence outline, of course, uses complete sentences for each heading and subheading. The sentence outline is more formal and takes more time and thought; the advantage is that it requires more careful thinking. Both topic and sentence outlines are the same in every other respect.

The outline as used in the writing of papers is composed of these parts:

Central Idea: This is one complete sentence that expresses the principal idea that the writer is trying to explain or discuss. The central or main idea should break down into the chief supporting points which will be given in the outline; the supporting points should add up to the central idea.

Supporting Points: The supporting points are the ideas that demonstrate or prove the central idea. There should be enough supporting points so that the main idea will be adequately explained. Only points which are needed to explain the central idea should be used.

Conclusion: The conclusion is the writer's evaluation of the main idea based on the supporting points. It is never a supporting point of the central idea.

The most commonly used outline form both for writing of papers and for taking of notes is as follows:

Large Roman numerals	I. — (Main headings)
Capitals	A. — (Most important subheadings)
	B. —
Arabic numbers	1. — (Subheadings of secondary importance)
	2. —
Small letters	a. — (Subheadings third in importance)
	b. —

Watch for these things in outlining:

1. Be sure that all parts of each subdivision are of equal importance.

2. Use parallel structure for headings in the same series. For example:

WRONG

A. Two uses of oxygen
   1. Oxidation of food (noun phrase)
   2. Oxygen purifies drinking water by oxidizing waste matter (Sentence)

RIGHT

A. Two uses of oxygen
   1. Oxidation of food (noun phrase)
   2. Purification of drinking water (noun phrase)

3. Main headings should either stand alone or be divided into two or more parts.

AN OUTLINE FOR A TERM PAPER

Students often have difficulty in seeing how the parts of the outline combine to form a pattern for the written expression of their ideas. The following is a concrete example of the use of a topic outline for a term paper. It was prepared by a student for an American History course. Although it is not necessarily a perfect outline, it is an example of careful work by an undergraduate student:

WILLIAM RANDOLPH HEARST
AND YELLOW JOURNALISM

Central Idea: This paper will give some of the highlights in the origin and development of yellow journalism in America and will show the important role played by William Randolph Hearst in this phase of American history.

I. Background of yellow journalism
  A. Joseph Pulitzer
    1. Brief background and entrance into newspaper work
    2. Pulitzer's purchases of the St. Louis *Post-Dispatch* and the New York *World*
  B. Pulitzer's creation of a New Journalism
    1. The six-part formula of the New Journalism
    2. Sensationalism
II. Hearst and the rise and fall of yellow journalism
  A. William Randolph Hearst
    1. Brief biography and entrance into newspaper business
    2. Purchase of the San Francisco *Examiner* and the New York *Morning Journal*

3. Development of the *Journal*
   into a sensational newspaper
B. The war between the *Journal*
   and the *World*
   1. The new Sunday journalism
   2. Arthur Brisbane's editorials
C. Journalistic jingoism: the Span-
   ish-American War
D. Yellow journalism at its height
E. Decline of yellow journalism
F. Permanent effects of the yellow
   press on modern journalism
   1. Banner headlines
   2. Many pictures
   3. The Sunday supplement
III. Hearst's chief contributions to
American journalism
A. Use of extreme sensationalism
   to attract readers
B. Development of newspaper
   chains

One of the best ways to use outlining
to assist you in learning and remembering is in organizing your notes—lecture,
reading, and research—so that your attention will be focussed on the main
points. This will be discussed in the
sections which follow.

TAKING NOTES

Lectures

In the process of being educated, the
student encounters a variety of teaching
methods. One of these methods is the
lecture which is an effective way of
covering material rapidly, crystallizing
key concepts, and elaborating on important points. However, from the
learner's standpoint, the lecture method
has serious limitations. It utilizes the

auditory avenue of learning, usually excluding other sensory avenues.

If visual and auditory devices are
combined, as in a motion picture or
lecture demonstration, the ability to
learn increases three or four times.
When visual and auditory materials are
combined, not only has each been used
for its own value but an extra factor has
been added to the learning process.

Since much of the material to be
learned in college will come from lectures, how can one get the most from
this method of teaching?

First, listen carefully to what is said.
Concentrate on the instructor's ideas.
Develop the ability to decide quickly,
as you listen, which are the most important points being made.

*Second, utilize the kinesthetic or
muscular response.* Some people, when
asked to spell a word, will say, "If I
can just write it, I'll remember it."
They are using a motor response, and
they can feel the words because they
recall through movement. By writing
down important lecture points in your
own words, you are not only gaining
valuable study material, you are utilizing muscle systems and establishing
motor patterns. Just as we learn to ice
skate or drive a nail with a hammer,
so can we also learn words through
movements.

*Third, look at notes and interpret
them carefully.* Read and review lecture notes as soon after class as possible to correct or clarify certain points
and to fix in your mind the essential
meaning of the teacher's lecture.

To sum up, if a student wishes to
obtain the most from a lecture, he will
listen attentively; he will write down

in his own words the information that seems most important; and he will re-read and review the notes to fix the concepts in his mind and keep the ideas fresh.

Taking effective lecture notes. How should lecture notes be taken? Here are some rules that may help:

1. Study the assignment before the lecture; this will provide a mental framework which will help ideas presented by the teacher to form a pattern.

2. Be prepared to take notes as soon as the instructor ·begins his lecture. Have your notebook open at the proper page and your pen ready.

3. Put notes down in outline form. Use capitals and small letters, numbers and indentations to show subdivisions.

4. Listen for clues (voice inflection, topic sentences, titles, key words, repetition of ideas, summaries) to the main points, then write these points down in brief summary statements. Jot down lesser ideas in their logical order. If the speaker rambles, outline accordingly.

5. Skip unnecessary words and don't worry about grammar. Use short cuts. Drop suffixes like *-tion* and *-ing*. Other

tricks similar to these can be invented, but be certain your notes will be understandable when read later. Shorthand is good if one does not use too much. Be sure it will be readable and will make sense later.

6. Leave lots of empty space on the page. Avoid heavy blocks of words and writing over words. Use very little underscoring, sidescoring, and other indications of emphasis.

7. Try to improve your notetaking skill so you can take neat, clear notes that will need few revisions.

8. Most important, develop the habit of listening with the intention of making outline notes. Practice will heighten attentiveness and help to develop skill in handling ideas. Remember, every word cannot be taken down. Notes should be an aid to remembering the *main* ideas; however, enough must be written down to recall the ideas accurately when the notes are cold.

9. Keep notes for all classes together in a loose-leaf notebook which is organized into subject areas by index tabs. The best size notebook paper is 8½" x 11"; this allows plenty of room for writing freedom. It is best to use only one side of the paper for notes; the other side may be used for comments or any extra material which may be pertinent to the subject of the lecture.

Reading Notes

Marking a book. The most important requirement is to have a book that you can mark. You should not mark library books; you should not mark books that belong to someone else.

Marking a book by underlining or any other way does not destroy its value; rather, marking enhances the book's usefulness by making it a part of you. After you have put down the first few marks in a book that you own, you have an exhilarating feeling of collaboration with the author.

Students often will not write in a book because they feel it will lower its resale value. If a student has no real desire to communicate with the author and select useful ideas from the discussion, then for him the purpose of the book is not to get the most *from it*, but to get the most *for it* at a second-hand store.

A book should be thought of as an author's expression of *his* ideas. He has made his information available to you; your job is to find ways to grasp the ideas that are presented. You can agree or disagree with them, but you should assimilate them as additional information about a particular subject. The end result is that you become the possessor of the ideas, not just the book.

If an idea impresses you, it should be marked so it can be quickly recognized. Your symbols added to the other printed material help to make the meaning clear to you.

There is no one correct way of marking a book. Your unique way may be just as effective as any that could be recommended. However, you must remember to be consistent in the method of marking you use. You will then be able to understand the meanings of the symbols at all times just as you understand word meanings. Following are some suggestions for marking which might help you get more meaning from your reading:

Use a pencil for all marking so mistakes can be erased. Before doing any underlining, read the chapter at least once. Underline sparingly—usually only key words and phrases; underline whole sentences only when they are very important.

Main points:	<u>mark heavily</u> or <u>with two lines</u>
Sub-points:	<u>mark with one line</u>
Points you disagree with or doubt:	use question mark (?)
A <u>word</u> or phrase that is (not clear) or new to you:	circle word or phrase
Points to be emphasized:	mark with an asterisk (*), slash (/) or check mark (✓)
To emphasize statements already underlined:	place vertical lines at margin ┃
Related points made by author elsewhere in the book:	place page numbers in margin
Your discussion of a concept:	write in the margin or top or bottom of page
A series of facts to be remembered:	indicate by circled numbers—① ② ③

A section of a marked textbook page.[1]

OVERCOMING OF FEARS

①- Series of facts

A fear situation can be <u>overcome</u> by ²disuse, understanding the elements that created the threat, and ③realizing that they no longer apply when one becomes an adult. This can be done either by <u>verbal appeal</u> or <u>by</u>

Emphasis ┃<u>realizing that the pattern of social limitation is a better or improved way of behaving towards the threat situation.</u> Fears may disappear or be to some extent <u>reduced or eliminated</u> by forgetting, disuse, or distraction.

New term A method of (negative adaptation) has been used in some cases quite effectively. In this type of therapy the subject is sent through the fear experience, and, if he finds that no harm is produced to the organism, he is somewhat able to overcome the fear. This method has been employed in a situation where a person has been hurt while flying or has seen someone else sustain bodily injury. He is immediately taken up in a plane so that the fear is not magnified. The same type of reduction of a fear situation is utilized when a structural steel worker falls from great heights to his death. The men break in unison and then go back on the job in order to remove the fear.

┃   <u>Fears</u> can also be <u>eliminated</u> or become <u>less severe</u> by means of <u>reconditioning.</u> If a certain environmental situation creates a fear, a <u>new type of reaction</u> can be produced. Pavlov's classic experiment in <u>conditioning</u> in which he presented food to the dog and created a salivary response was an example of this.

Try marking this book. A start has been màde below to show what might be done.

Outlining a textbook. Outlining the reading done in a textbook can be of great benefit to a student, because he must figure out the general structure of the author's discussion and find the main ideas and the points that enlarge those ideas. This compels the student to read actively with a purpose, and in addition he is learning by doing which brings about better retention.

Using your own words in an outline to condense what the book says is a form of recitation. It is a way of finding out if you can express the ideas in the book. Besides, it is an excellent way of reviewing, because thought is required to condense the material and focus on the main points. Outlining a text makes reviewing easier, because (1)* the outline acts as a condensed guide, and (2)* the student is aided in recalling the main points previously learned.

A sentence outline is usually the most effective type to use in textbook outlining. Look for the principal ideas in the sections under the textbook headings and use these ideas as the main outline headings. The points that support and amplify these ideas will become the subheadings.

At the beginning of your textbook outline, be sure to write the book title, chapter number, and chapter title. Keep all your outlines together in your notebook in correct chapter order in the proper subject areas.

Research Notes

Research notes are taken during the gathering of material for a term paper. After the student has decided on a general topic and done some preliminary reading, he should (1) compose a sentence (central idea) that states what he would like to do in his paper, and (2) make a rough outline. These two steps will help to conserve time by guiding and limiting the research program. Although both the central idea and the outline may be changed several times during the research and writing process, they will help to keep facts organized.

The first outline—often called a "scratch" outline—may consist of only a list of headings pertaining to the main topic. For instance, the student who prepared the outline on page 79 may have begun like this:

  I. Biography of Hearst
 II. History of yellow journalism
III. Characteristics of yellow journalism
IV. Effect of yellow journalism on American newspapers

As the student begins reading magazine articles and skimming through books guided by this simple list, he will immediately see ways of expanding and rearranging the outline into its final form.

The student has no idea as yet how much of the material he is accumulating will actually be used or how it will eventually be organized; therefore, it is best to use 3 x 5 or 4 x 6 cards for recording information, because they can be shuffled around and rearranged in any order desired.

At this time, two types of cards will be made—bibliography cards and note cards. Bibliography cards list *only* sources where information is found; note cards record the information with only brief source references. Since they are closely related, they may often be made out at the same time.

1. Bibliography cards. Each bibliography card contains *all* the information about *one* source—a book, magazine article, etc.—which might be useful in the writing of the paper. This source information should follow a definite bibliographical form (see examples following) since these cards will eventually be used for the bibliography at the end of the paper. Also, many teachers collect bibliography cards during the time the paper is being written and check them for form. The cards in the library card catalogue contain all the information needed for bibliography cards. See Chapter 6 for finding material in the library.

Forms for bibliography cards

I. Bibliography cards for books should include the following items which will be found on the library catalogue card:
 1. Complete library call number
 2. Author, last name first
 3. Title of book, underlined
 4. Place of publication
 5. Publisher
 6. Copyright date
 7. If book is edited, name of editor
 8. Location—either name of library or "Personal" if you own the book; this can be a great help if it is necessary to refer to the book again.
II. Bibliography cards for encyclopedia articles should include:
 1. Library call number
 2. If article is signed, name of author—otherwise, title of article

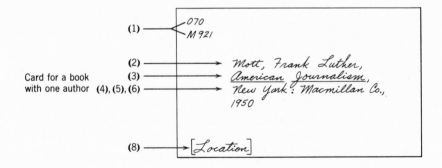

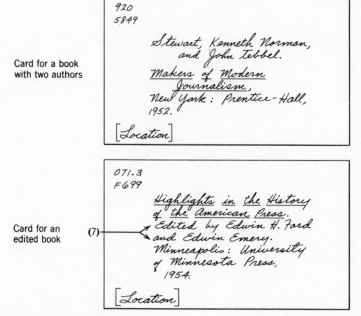

Card for a book with two authors

920
5849

Stewart, Kenneth Norman, and John Tebbel.
Makers of Modern Journalism,
New York: Prentice-Hall, 1952.
[Location]

Card for an edited book (7)

071.3
F699

Highlights in the History of the American Press.
Edited by Edwin H. Ford and Edwin Emery.
Minneapolis: University of Minnesota Press, 1954.
[Location]

3. Title of article, enclosed in quotation marks
4. Name of encyclopedia, underlined
5. Copyright date
6. Volume number in Roman numerals
7. Page numbers of article
8. Location

III. Bibliography cards for magazine or newspaper (periodical) articles should show the following facts:
1. Call number from a card from either the card catalogue or special periodical file in the library
2. Author (may not be given in newspaper articles)
3. Title of article
4. Name of periodical
5. Volume of magazine, if one is given
6. Date article appeared
7. Pages of the article; also, section of newspaper
8. Location

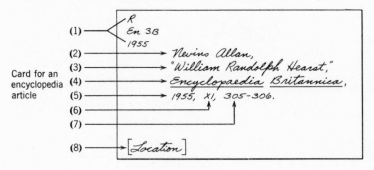

Card for an encyclopedia article

(1)
R
En 3B
1955
(2) Nevins Allan,
(3) "William Randolph Hearst,"
(4) Encyclopaedia Britannica,
(5) 1955, XI, 305-306.
(6)
(7)
(8) [Location]

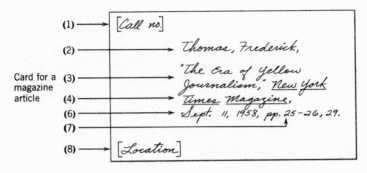

Card for a magazine article

(1) [Call no.]
(2) Thomas, Frederick,
(3) "The Era of Yellow Journalism," New York
(4) Times Magazine,
(6) Sept. 11, 1958, pp. 25-26, 29.
(7)
(8) [Location]

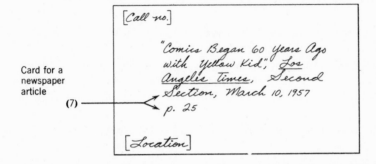

Card for a newspaper article

[Call no.]

"Comics Began 60 Years Ago with Yellow Kid," Los Angeles Times, Second Section, March 10, 1957

(7) p. 25

[Location]

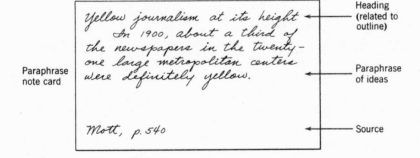

Paraphrase note card

Yellow journalism at its height
In 1900, about a third of the newspapers in the twenty-one large metropolitan centers were definitely yellow.

Mott, p. 540

Heading (related to outline)

Paraphrase of ideas

Source

Direct quotation note card

Arthur Brisbane's editorials
"As a writer, with these editorials, as an editor, with thorough grasp of what his kind of reader wanted, he came to typify yellow journalism in its last period of real power."

Ford and Emery, p. 283

Quotation marks clearly indicate direct quote

2. Note cards. Notetaking on cards generally consists of short summaries of the material read unless the notes are direct quotations. These summaries or paraphrases should be accurate and should include the main ideas and any details which seem important in expanding the topic chosen. The student should word his paraphrasing so it sounds natural and not like the original material with the words shifted around.

Since it is not possible or even necessary to actually read a large number of books when researching for a term paper, the student should train himself to find useful sections quickly. This can be done by analyzing the index and table of contents and by rapid scanning of the pages.

Remember these important facts about taking research notes:

1. Only one note is to be put on each card.
2. The heading on each card should be related to one of the outline headings.
3. The source of each note should be given along with the exact page number.
4. Enough notes should be taken from each article or book so it will not be necessary to look them up again.
5. Notes should be limited only to the topic being considered.
6. Enclose each direct quotation in quotation marks so there will be no later confusion about whether the reference is in the student's or the author's words.

7. Every direct quotation must be acknowledged as such and credit given to the author; plagiarism is regarded by instructors as a serious offense.
8. It is best to use a limited number of direct quotes in a paper.
9. Each note should indicate whether it is someone's opinion or an actual fact.
10. The student must learn to evaluate sources of information. All writing varies as to type and purpose. For instance, data in an encyclopedia is more generalized and less detailed than that given in a magazine or book devoted to one subject. It should also be remembered that each author writes from his own point of view. Although two authors may write about the same subject, the result may be entirely different.

The student should also evaluate the reliability of the source. Is the author considered by others to be an authority on the subject? Has he proven his knowledge in some way—perhaps by successfully filling an important position in this field? Does he seem biased in his opinions? Has the book or article been written recently enough to give the latest information?

Reference

1. Lyle Tussing, *Psychology for Better Living*, New York, John Wiley and Sons, 1959, p. 43.

Test Yourself on Chapter 7

1. T F   Topic and sentence outlines are different in every way but one.
2. T F   The conclusion of an outline is usually a supporting point of the central idea.
3. T F   It is important to use parallel structure for headings in the same series.
4. T F   Main headings in an outline can either stand alone or have one or more subheadings.
5. T F   The supporting points prove the central idea.
6. Plagiarism in a term paper should be avoided by ————.
7. In order to obtain the most from lectures, a student should (1)————; (2)———— ; (3)————.
8. Outlining a textbook can be a valuable learning aid because ————————
   ————————.
9. During a lecture the student should listen for clues to important points. Some of these clues are (1)———— (2)———— (3)————.
10. Marking a book makes it more valuable because ————————.
11. All the information necessary for bibliography cards will be found in ————————
   ————————.
12. The heading on each note card should be related to ————————.
13. Bibliography cards contain ————; note cards contain ————.
14. In order to guide and limit his research for a term paper, the student should do two things: (1)————; (2)————.
15. To find the useful parts of books when doing research, the student should ———— and ————.

Exercises in Outlining

I. Develop a sentence outline of this chapter as if it were the subject of a term paper.

II. Make a text outline for study of either this chapter or any one of the preceding chapters; use a topic outline form.

8
PRESENTING WRITTEN AND ORAL MATERIAL

WRITTEN ASSIGNMENTS

Few college students will become professional writers, but all students will find it necessary to write understandably—in college, in business, and in their social lives. In writing, as in speaking, the desired result is communication. Clear, effective written communication may be achieved by learning and applying the basic rules of grammar, punctuation, and spelling.

One very effective way to improve one's writing is to use good grammar in everyday speech so that expressing ideas well becomes a habit. Another way is to look critically at everything one writes and try to catch all minor errors in grammar and spelling. College students are expected to be able to spell correctly, and many teachers deduct valuable points for misspelled words.

Those who are unsure of their punctuation, grammar, or spelling should obtain a good English composition book and a dictionary and use them constantly. A condensed list of the rules of punctuation will be found at the end of this section.

General Requirements for Written Assignments

College writing assignments are usually reading reports, themes, and term papers. Before beginning any writing project, the student must know what the teacher expects as far as length and form are concerned. Is the paper to be limited to a certain number of words? What form, if any, has the teacher specified for division of the paper (chapters, section headings, etc.), footnoting, bibliography, introduction and conclusion?

The student must also know the date on which the assignment is due. He should allow plenty of time before the deadline to complete the paper so he will avoid poor writing and grade penalties for lateness.

There are certain general concepts which are basic to all three types of writing:

1. *Controlling purpose*—The central idea must be specific and clearly defined.

2. *Logical arrangement and development of material*—Develop an outline and work from it. (See Chapter 7 for a discussion of outlining.)

TUSSING. W-60

3. *Principles of good composition*—Using an outline as an internal struc-

ture upon which to build a piece of writing will help to develop these principles:

a. Unity: All parts of a composition should contribute to a unified whole—all ideas should be related to the central idea.

b. Coherence: There should be an orderly arrangement of the sections of the composition.

c. Emphasis: Stress should be placed on the most important ideas.

d. Adequate development: The main ideas should be sufficiently developed.

4. *Conciseness and clarity*

a. Eliminate unnecessary words and ideas. For example:

the question as to whether—whether

he *is a man who*—he

there is no doubt *that*—no doubt

b. Use clear, simple language; avoid flowery, unclear expresions. Compare the following:

My house pet is stupendous in his outstanding knowledge and ability.

My dog is very intelligent.

5. *Revising and correcting*
a. Proofread the entire paper carefully.
b. Test each sentence for clearness of language and adequate development of ideas.
c. Cut out any words or sentences which interfere with clarity of thought or logical sequence of ideas.
d. If necessary, shift sentences or paragraphs around to achieve a better progression of ideas.
e. Check bibliography and footnotes (if paper has them) for correctness of form.
f. Make a very careful check of spelling and grammar.
g. If possible, type the final copy of the paper.

h. It is a good idea to make a carbon copy of the paper since it may be useful in the future as a reference.

TYPES OF WRITING

Reading Report

A reading report might be a report on a book, an article, a short story, or a poem. It should be concise and stress the important problems and facts. Teachers generally look for these things in a reading report:

1. *A brief summary of the work read*
2. *The form and manner of presentation:* for poetry—the type of poem, length, rhyme scheme, meter, etc.; for prose—whether it is a short story, novel, play, article, essay, autobiography, etc.; for prose or poetry, some comments about writing style—understandable, flowery, moving, etc.
3. *The student's reaction to the work:* the ideas or feelings conveyed.
4. *The importance of the work:* critics may be consulted (but not copied) to help the student form an intelligent opinion.

Theme

A theme is a composition which develops an idea usually suggested by the teacher. Theme writing may be divided into four general classifications:
1. *Description:* a word picture of a place, person, or scene which the writer has experienced or imagined.
2. *Narration:* the story of an event or one part of a large event.
3. *Exposition:* facts and ideas meant to inform, explain, or convince the reader.
4. *Argumentation:* similar to exposition, but intended to convince and persuade rather than explain.

These four areas tend to overlap, but are classified according to the type which predominates.

Term Paper

A term paper presents a student's original idea which he derived from thinking and reading about a particular subject; it is a composition (usually of about 1,500 to 3,000 words) which is organized by methods recommended by learned individuals. These methods for organizing and composing a term paper include the following areas:

1. *Selecting a subject:* The topic should be interesting to the student; it should be narrow enough so it may be adequately developed in the assigned number of words; there should be enough reference material available (usually at least five sources); the topic should be defined as clearly as possible in a positive statement called the thesis sentence.

2. *Gathering information:* Research notes should be recorded on cards (3 x 5 or 4 x 6); each card should be used for one reference. Details of notetaking are found in Chapter 7.

3. *Building an outline:* State the central idea of the paper in a thesis sentence; arrange the note cards in the order in which the material is to be presented; the term paper should be composed so that it follows the outline—frequently the outline serves as a table of contents (depending upon the wishes of the teacher).

The final draft of the term paper should contain the following:

1. Title page
2. Outline
3. Text of the paper
4. Bibliography (on a separate page following the last page of the text)

The student will make a wise investment by purchasing a form book which describes in detail the writing of a term paper and also includes a sample outline and paper. Teachers may recommend books of this type which they feel are dependable and helpful. Several of these publications which are often recommended are:

Cooper, Charles W., and Edmund J. Robins, *The Term Paper,* Stanford, Stanford University Press, 1947.

Coyle, William, *Research Papers,* New York, The Odyssey Press, 1960.

Sears, Donald A., *Harbrace Guide to the Library and the Research Paper,* New York, Harcourt, Brace and World, Inc., 1960.

Yaggy, Elinor, *How to Write Your Term Paper,* Los Altos, Howard Chandler, 1958.

PUNCTUATION

Punctuation marks are used to clarify the meaning of a piece of writing; any punctuation that does not make the meaning clearer should be eliminated. *Punctuation should help in reading and prevent misreading.*

Period

After a declarative sentence (a positive statement): I am going home at five o'clock.

After an imperative sentence (a command): Bring the lamp over here.

To indicate ellipsis (word omission) in a quotation—3 periods; 4 periods when ellipsis comes at end of sentence: "Fourscore and seven years ago our fathers brought forth . . . a new nation. . . ."

After abbreviations: Dr., Jr., etc., Mrs., A.M., P.M.

Question Mark

At the end of direct questions: Are you attending college this semester?

After each question in a series: Will you buy it? or you? or anyone?

Exclamation Point

To indicate surprise, admiration, or other strong emotion: How dreadful!

Colon

After a complete statement which introduces a list of items or ideas: The list of supplies included the following items: pins, needles, scissors, and thread.

To introduce long formal quotations: Clarence Darrow rose from his chair and said: "Ladies and gentlemen of the jury, I will begin my summation of this case by saying that. . . ."

Before concrete illustrations that clarify a statement: There is only one way to solve this problem: send him more money.

After the salutation of a business or formal letter: Dear Sir: or To Whom It May Concern:

Semicolon

Between independent clauses in place of coordinate conjunctions: An independent clause is a group of words that can stand alone because it expresses a complete thought; the coordinate conjunctions *and, or, nor, but,* and *for* are used to connect independent clauses.

Between sentences joined by coordinate conjunctions when the sentences are long and contain much punctuation: The trip was planned by Tom, Phil, Jim, and Norman; but Mary, Judy, Kathleen, and Joan were allowed to join the boys because they promised to bring food.

Comma

To separate independent clauses joined by coordinate conjunctions: Dinner was over, but everyone lingered at the table.

To prevent misreading of a sentence: Below, the hills looked soft and velvety.

To set off nonrestrictive phrases or clauses (additional thought or information): The president of our Club, John Everett, will introduce the speaker.

After each part of a series of three or more words, phrases, or numbers used with *and, or,* or *nor:* My father, mother, and grandmother came to my graduation.

After introductory modifying phrases or clauses: On arriving at the airport, Mary discovered her plane had just left. / To get home on time, we had to leave by 4:30 P.M.

To separate parts of a date, an address, geographical names, and to set off titles after names: They were married on July 22, 1955, and have two children. / My new address is 17113 Flower Avenue, Los Angeles, California. / Seattle, Washington, is a beautiful city. / Thomas Fox, Ph.D., has published a new book.

To set off words or names used in direct address: I think, John, that you are wrong. / Children, it's time to go to sleep.

Quotation Marks

To enclose exact words of a speaker or writer: "Can you visit me next week?" asked Mrs. Haggerty. / The speaker at tonight's meeting emphasized the importance of "a warm, friendly home atmosphere."

To enclose titles of short works—articles, songs, short stories, short poems, speeches, one-act plays, and chapters of books: The title of the first chapter of his new book is "How Shall We Begin?" / William Jennings Bryan's "Cross of Gold" speech is considered the greatest one he ever made.

Commas and periods placed inside quotation marks, semicolon outside; question mark and exclamation mark placed inside quotation marks when they concern only the material quoted, outside when they apply to the sentence as a whole: "Ann," the teacher said, "please read your composition to the class." / Father had often said, "I will never vote for a Republican"; yet in the last election he voted the straight Republican ticket. / The hobo asked, "Have you any work I can do?" / Are you sure the hobo asked, "Have you any work I can do"?

Parentheses

To set off material used for comment or explanation but having little bearing on the main thought: The campers took food (whatever they liked) for one day.

To enclose figures repeated for accuracy or used for enumeration: The library card catalogue (see Chapter 6) is a great help to college students. / Please include (1) your full name, (2) your address, and (3) the school last attended.

Dash

Instead of parentheses for informality; to mark a sudden break or abrupt change in thought: I've decided to— but you wouldn't be interested.

Instead of commas or parentheses to give more emphasis: At the age of three —incredible as it sounds—Gary was an excellent swimmer.

ORAL REPORTS

In preparing and presenting an oral report, some basic ideas should be kept in mind. The most important thing to remember is that a talk given before a group of people is merely an enlarged conversation. Face your audience with the feeling that they are a friendly group of people who are interested in what you have to say. Speak to them in a conversational tone of voice, rather than an oratorical one.

The people in the audience want to learn about the things you know. It is up to you to express your ideas in such a way that they will want to listen and understand the important things you have to say.

In order to interest others, the topic must first of all be of interest to you. You should not deliver just a collection of dry facts—show that you understand what you are talking about and that what you are saying is important to them. A speaker who merely reports facts and figures won't create much in-

terest in his audience; he is quite likely to lose their attention because they cannot see how the material is important to them. You, as the speaker, are the connecting link between *what* you know and *why* what you know is important to your listeners.

It has been said that an after-dinner speaker should be good, be brief, and be gone. However, the length of a class report will depend upon the length of the assignment and also upon the time limit (if any) set by the teacher. The secret of being good and being brief is to boil down a large amount of material and present only the choice, interesting, essential information.

Making an outline will help you to organize your ideas and information so you will be able to present them clearly and logically. This will prevent rambling in a disorganized fashion and your audience will be able to follow your thoughts easily.

Oral reports should begin with an introductory statement, proceed to the body of the topic, and end with closing remarks which sum up the main ideas.

The introductory material should catch the interest of the audience. Do not apologize for the talk you are about to give, and do not start with a cut and dried statement. Compare these two beginning statements for a talk about safety:

"The topic I have been assigned is 'Safety,' and I'm going to talk about traffic accidents."

"One of you will be taken to the hospital this year! Someone from this class will have a serious traffic accident, if my statistics are right."

After breaking through the apathy of the audience with an interesting beginning, you hold their attention by your dynamic presentation of facts on the subject. Look alive! In this manner you can overcome any "ho-hum—so what?" attitude they might have.

The closing statements of an oral report should sum up the ideas which you have presented. This is called "restatement"; it is very important because (1) repeating important points will help the audience to remember them, and (2) your listeners are left with a clear picture of the main thoughts in your report.

If you feel nervous before giving your talk, take a few deep breaths. This slows down the breathing and helps to create a feeling of confidence in your ability to present your material well. A smile will sometimes help to relieve tension and will also make the audience more receptive to what you are going to say.

Remind yourself that there is really nothing to fear. It is not likely that anyone is going to throw anything or hurt you in any way while you are

giving a class report! Your biggest fear is probably that you may not be as good a speaker as you would like to be. This, of course, can be eliminated by thorough preparation.

A short outline on a 3 x 5 card held in the palm of the hand may act as a small crutch to reassure the speaker who fears he may forget a point. If a report is long and more notes are permitted, the outline can be made longer and more detailed. However, the student should avoid burying his nose in the paper during his presentation.

In some situations when accuracy is desired, reading may be permitted; but it should be realized that concentrating on the written material may cause the speaker to lose contact with his surroundings. When you must read a written report, be sure to maintain eye contact with the audience. This will keep them aware of you as a per-

son and interested in what you are saying.

To sum up, we might say that in giving an oral report you are doing these things:

1. You are demonstrating your ability to assemble a group of related facts and arrange them in the order of their importance to you.

2. You are presenting this accumulation of thoughts in a manner which will make them interesting and meaningful to your listeners.

Remember to be yourself when you give a talk; be friendly and sincere, and your audience will react in the same way.

CLASS DISCUSSION AND PARTICIPATION

Many students find it difficult to speak out in a classroom because they are afraid of saying something which might be ridiculed. Actually, observation of the comments made by students who often take part in class discussions will show they do not always say the "right" thing or the "smart" thing. But these students—and the whole class—

learn either from being corrected by the teacher or from a discussion arising from their comments.

If you are to benefit from a class discussion, you must take an active part in it. You may not be very interested at first, but by forcing yourself to take part, you will find yourself becoming interested and even excited. Your thinking will be stimulated so that you will leave class with some new ideas and perhaps some questions in mind. This will help you in studying the assignment; also, these questions may be the basis for another class discussion.

Although it is usually the instructor's job to keep the classroom talk from wandering too far from the original topic, the students must build the structure of the discussion and keep it moving. Reading the assignment before coming to class helps to give a student self-confidence; he feels that, should he be called upon in a class discussion, he will be able to contribute intelligently. He is also more likely to volunteer and to keep the talk moving.

Building a class discussion may be compared to building a house. It is not possible to build a complete structure in a single day. The foundation is worked on first; then the rooms are laid out. Later, more detail is added, such as the color of the walls and floor and the type and placement of furniture. In a discussion, the same procedure is followed; the main idea is outlined, then broken up into divisions, and these in turn are examined and evaluated.

Each person who contributes to a discussion adds to the structure or gives emphasis to what has already been said. Just as a house is never finally and completely furnished and decorated, so is a class discussion never really completed.

Test Yourself on Chapter 8

1. What is the secret of giving a short, interesting, talk? ———————.
2. The general concepts which are basic to reading reports, themes, and term papers are: (1)——— (2)——— (3)——— (4)——— (5)———.
3. A talk given before a group of people is only an ———————————.
4. What is the purpose of punctuation? ———————————————.
5. How is an outline helpful in preparing a talk? ————————————.

Punctuation Exercise

Insert punctuation where it is missing. A key will be found after the last exercise in this chapter.

1. The title of this chapter is Presenting Written and Oral Material.
2. Dr. Sigmund Freud pronounced Froid lived from 1865 to 1939.
3. Positive reasons for the study of human adjustment include the following first finding ways to relieve maladjustments second gaining a knowledge of human behavior to help us understand ourselves and others third knowing ourselves better how we developed our abilities and limitations how we can meet and solve problems.
4. What would your answer be if you were asked What does college mean to you
5. Philosophy may be defined as a person's formal or informal ordered or disordered consistent or inconsistent and conscious or unconscious assumptions about the nature of truth.
6. Professor Templeton the philosophy teacher said Philosophy has to do with the nature of being or reality
7. He added that philosophy is the study of the nature of knowledge and it is also concerned with what knowing is.

Self-Appraisal Tests

Grammar and spelling have not been discussed in this chapter. However, the tests in this secton should help you evaluate some of your weaknesses and strengths in these areas.

Grammar

This exercise deals with some common grammatical errors. Write the correct word in the blank after each sentence. Answers will be found after the last exercise.

1. A book of names (is, are) very useful to new parents. ————
2. In every part of the United States (is, are) people who have been unemployed for many months. ————
3. Marcia is one of those women who (like, likes) to be on committees. ————
4. My brother and (I, me) were born ten minutes apart. ————
5. She was the one individual (who, whom) I thought could be trusted. ————

6. No one could ride the horse but (I, me).   _____

7. I was quite upset at (him, his) telling me that my father was ill.   _____

8. George and Anne can't play badminton as well as (us, we).   _____

9. (Most, Almost) all of the employees went on strike.   _____

10. Mr. Carmichael felt (bad, badly) about discharging old Mr. Jones.   _____

11. This new textbook is the (best, better) of the two books.   _____

12. Between you and (I, me) the party was a failure.   _____

13. Either the father or the mother of each child (is, are) required to give
    (his, their) permission.   _____

14. Everyone should do (his, their) job as well as (he, they) can.   _____

15. The boy looked (good, well) in his new suit.   _____

Spelling

Following is a list of fifty common words which college students often misspell. Have you had trouble with them?

absorption	dictionary	grammar	neither	rhythm
accommodate	discipline	hypocrisy	noticeable	seize
aggravate	eighth	immediately	nuclear	sergeant
arctic	embarrass	independent	omission	susceptible
believe	exceed	jealousy	origin	transferred
benefited	existence	knowledge	parallel	tyranny
career	February	license	personnel	undoubtedly
conscientious	forty	loneliness	politician	usually
criticism	friend	mischievous	quizzes	vengeance
descendant	government	municipal	referred	writing

Make your own list of words which you often spell incorrectly. Read them carefully aloud, a syllable at a time, then write them a number of times. You will be forming both mental and muscular patterns to help you remember.

Words I Frequently Misspell

This exercise contains more words which seem to be difficult for college students. Some of these words are spelled correctly and some are not. In the blank provided, place a √ if the spelling is right and an X if it is wrong. Check with your dictionary to see how many you have right.

_____1. achievment	_____11. environment	_____21. murmer
_____2. athletic	_____12. exorbitant	_____22. occured
_____3. basicly	_____13. fasinate	_____23. parliament
_____4. Britain	_____14. finally	_____24. recognize
_____5. calender	_____15. guage	_____25. sieze
_____6. changable	_____16. height	_____26. sophmore
_____7. consentrate	_____17. hindrence	_____27. tragedy
_____8. decision	_____18. indispensible	_____28. unecessary
_____9. disapear	_____19. leisure	_____29. villain
_____10. dying	_____20. maintenance	_____30. wierd

seperate

Punctuation Key	Grammar Key
1. "Presenting . . . Material."	1. is
2. Dr. Sigmund Freud (pronounced Froid)	2. are
3. following:	3. like
first, . . . maladjustments;	4. I
second, . . . others;	5. who
third, . . . better—	6. me
developed,	7. his
limitations,	8. we
4. asked, "What . . . you?"	9. Almost
5. informal,	10. bad
disordered,	11. better
inconsistent,	12. me
6. Templeton,	13. is
teacher,	his
said,	14. his
"philosophy . . . reality."	he
7. knowledge,	15. good

9
TAKING EXAMS

PREPARING FOR EXAMINATIONS

The best preparation for examinations is keeping up with assignments and studying regularly. Another excellent way you can help yourself is to take time for a short review of all subjects at least once a month. An hour or two spent looking over the material that has been covered in each course will keep it fresh in your mind; it will also cut down on the time needed for review before tests. Even more important, when the final exam period arrives, you will know the subject matter thoroughly and will be able to avoid last-minute cramming.

The time spent in reviewing for an exam should not cut into the time scheduled for studying other subjects. It is a good idea to set up a review schedule when a test is announced. In addition to the time already set aside for studying this particular subject, you may decide you need to use some of your free hours for review. However, be careful not to eliminate your recreation altogether. Relaxing and "getting away" from school work are also important.

Some Helpful Ways To Review

1. It is not always necessary to re-read the text and notes in detail. Many times it is better to select the main points under the headings of each chapter and see if you understand them. If you are uncertain of some points, re-read the section which explains them.

2. Some students make a summary or outline of all their notes on a subject. This includes notes of all kinds—reading, lecture, etc. The effort involved in making this outline is an excellent way of fixing important facts in the mind. It should be read over a number of times and the main points recited aloud.

3. Try to anticipate the questions the teacher might ask. Check the points he seemed to emphasize in his lectures or class discussions. As you review the material under each heading, try to figure out what kind of questions could be asked about it.

4. Whether a test is objective or essay, thorough study and review is necessary. The only differences to consider in studying for either type of test is that an objective test might call for more details, while an essay test might emphasize relationships among different aspects of the course material.

Cramming

The most ineffective method of studying is cramming—trying to learn everything at one time the night before an exam. The loss of sleep and the disorganization of daily living habits may produce feelings of nervousness, tiredness, and confusion. The worst result of cramming is that the facts which have been so frantically accumulated will disappear in a short time.

However, there is a review technique which might be thought of as a form of cramming. It can be very effective if used *after* all the material has been studied and reviewed during regularly scheduled study sessions. The final study period before the exam may be used for an intensive, overall review of everything you have studied. This last-minute review, along with a good night's sleep, can help you to remember the material, especially troublesome points.

TAKING EXAMINATIONS

There are a few important and effective steps that any student can take to improve his examination grade.

1. Make a 30-second survey of the exam to see how many questions there are, how difficult each one is, and the grade value given to each question. Then budget your time, allowing the most time to questions which have the highest value. An average student may answer 3 to 5 true-false questions a minute and 2 to 4 multiple choice questions a minute. Plan to take all the time assigned for the test.

2. If all the questions are of equal value, it is better to answer the easier ones first; as you write, you may remember the answers to the more difficult ones.

3. Make use of returned examinations. Study the questions missed; analyze the wrong answers.

Taking Essay Exams

a. *Read and follow all instructions.* Know the meaning of cue words such as these:

Analyze—to examine critically so as to show essential features.

Compare—to show points of likeness and difference between two or more things.

Contrast—to show difference or unlikenesses between two or more things.

Define—to give a clear, undetailed, but precise meaning.

Elaborate—to develop a theme or idea in greater detail.

Evaluate—to appraise carefully, giving both the positive and negative aspects.

Explain—to clarify and interpret the details of a problem, theory, etc.

Illustrate—to explain or clarify by giving an example.

List—to set down under each other a series of facts, dates, words, names, etc.

Outline—to organize facts by arranging them in a series of headings and subheadings to show relationships.

b. Organize the answer; do not write haphazardly about the first idea that comes to mind.

c. Write enough, giving all details asked for.

d. Write legibly. Use ink. Be sure questions are numbered correctly.

e. Read and check what you have written before you turn it in.

Taking Objective Exams

a. *True-False:* Guess if there is no heavy penalty on T-F questions.

b. *Completion:* Don't leave blanks. An answer you think is wrong may be acceptable. Go back and check over the doubtful questions with a fresh viewpoint; this may eliminate the mental block.

c. *Matching:* Answer the easy ones first. This reduces the choice for hard ones.

d. *Multiple Choice:* Cross out what is obviously wrong, thus reducing the choice. Mark only one.

Taking Science Exams

Exams in science courses are different in some ways from those given in other courses. In addition to the usual objective and essay tests, laboratory tests are given. One life science instructor, Mary Sidey of the Life Science Department at El Camino College, California, gives her students a sheet at the beginning of the semester on which she describes the types of tests given in her course. Many teachers follow the same general pattern which she uses:

Lab Tests:

1. Short answer questions—identification of parts; functions; classification of specimens studied.

2. Pointing out structures you have dissected out on your own specimen.
3. Labelling diagrams or exact drawings of material studied.
4. LAB PRACTICALS—students enter a lab with stations set up around the room—one student goes to each station—he answers the question at that station, and then stands at that station, facing the front of the room until the bell rings to indicate that he is to move to the next station. Practical knowledge as to the actual material is tested in this fashion. *Don't learn from diagrams and then blame the specimen because it is not clear! THE SPECIMEN IS YOUR AUTHORITY.*

Lecture Tests:

1. Short answer type.
2. Short essay type.
3. I.B.M. MULTIPLE CHOICE QUESTIONS—choose one answer out of five.
   I.B.M. TRUE-FALSE—if any part of the statement is false, it is all false.
   I.B.M. MULTIPLE CHOICE QUESTIONS—choose any number of answers for each question out of 15 choices. Matching questions come on this part of the test, e.g., matching mammals with their Orders, or putting insects in their correct Order.

Quite often, instructors in science courses use a point system for determining final grades. This can be helpful to the student because he knows the grade importance of each area of the course. Also, he knows where he stands during the semester, and he can see in which areas he needs to improve in order to bring up his grade. The following is an example of such a point system.

4 Lecture Tests @ 75 each	300
1 Mid-Term Lecture Test	100
1 Final Lecture Test	200
	———
	600 on lecture (approx.)
15 Lab Quizzes @ 20 each	300
1 Mid-Term Practical	50
1 Finals Practical	50
	———
	400 on lab (approx.)
Total Points in Course	800 to 1000 (approx.)

90–100%	A
80– 89%	B
65– 79%	C
55– 64%	D
0– 54%	F

Approximately 60% Lecture, 40% Laboratory, is the balance of points.

You should respect the instructor's judgment enough not to pressure him to change your "one point off" grade to the next highest. He knows if he has been too harsh and may change it on his own, but he is duty bound not to waver under pressure.

Make-Up Tests

Many instructors do not give make-up tests. They feel that students who are "sick" on the day an exam is given gain an unfair advantage by having extra time to study. Also, teachers are usually too busy to stop and give extra tests. Many schools have found that most make-ups are taken by students who eventually drop the course or fail it.

Even though your teachers give make-ups, it is best to develop the habit of being present when tests are given. Sometimes points are automatically subtracted for late tests, and often a different, perhaps more difficult, test is given. You may occasionally be tempted to get "sick" and put off an exam for a day or two, but try to remember it is to your advantage to take tests on time.

Test Yourself on Chapter 9

1. T F In studying for an exam, the text as well as all notes should always be reviewed in detail.

2. T F When answering completion questions, it is better to leave blanks than to put down an answer that may be wrong.

3. T F Objective tests require the same amount of review as essay tests.

4. T F If all questions on a test are equal in value, answer the easier ones first.

5. T F Cramming for exams is never effective.

6. Write the definitions for these important cue words:

Analyze ——————————
Elaborate ——————————
Evaluate ——————————
Illustrate ——————————
Outline ——————————

Use Returned Exams to Improve Your Grades

Utilize test papers which are returned to you. Keep them in the back of your notebook or in a separate notebook, dividing them by subject. Study the questions missed so you will understand why they are wrong; this can help you make better grades on final exams.

Do you find that you make certain consistent errors on exams? Are you marked down for poor spelling, illegible handwriting, or poor organization or ideas? Perhaps you are not paying enough attention to cue words. Make a list of any cue words not given in this chapter which have appeared on tests you have had; write the definitions. An occasional review of all cue words can be very helpful.

CUE WORDS   DEFINITIONS

Make notes of mistakes you have made on tests. Then write down ways you may help yourself to avoid these mistakes on future exams.

Predicting Exams Questions

One helpful way to study for a test is to try to decide what questions might be asked. You can try to remember what points the teacher emphasized in his lectures and what kinds of questions he has asked on past exams. Also, as you review the text material you can make notes on any points that seem especially important to you.

In this space, write out ten questions that might be asked on Chapter 2, "Learning and Study."

10

CONDITIONS AND TECHNIQUES RELATED TO THINKING AND LEARNING

THE NEED FOR MENTAL FLEXIBILITY

One of the greatest hindrances to learning is man's tendency toward non-flexible thinking. The ability to associate new ideas with previously learned material is greatly dependent upon a flexible mind. Quite often, a person cannot find an answer to a problem because he is not able to see how his past experiences and the knowledge that he has acquired are related to his present problem.

An "open mind"—one that is receptive to being shown that by a series of steps the outcome may be something different than previously anticipated— is one of the components of mental flexibility. However, *complete* "open-mindedness" would result in a lack of stability, and a person who reacted in this way would be considered fickle or inconsistent. But, at the other ex-

treme, a person with a "closed mind" is one who is set against any change because the "right" information has already been obtained; he has difficulty,

not in seeing and analyzing, but in integrating any new information because the answer has already been discovered.

When one's thinking is designated as "rigid," he may accept a new or different idea only if it fits a preconceived pattern. He is reluctant to recognize either variation or exception. In addition, there may be a need to channel, screen, and distort ideas in order to reach a preconceived outcome.

Some of the research done in the methods of previous mental structuring indicates that even though a problem may be relatively simple, the strength of the beliefs held about the information needed to resolve the problem and the methods of attack may act either as a catalyst to produce continuity of thinking or as a block to prevent it. Rokeach,[1] in his book *The Open and Closed Mind*, describes a simple problem with an imaginary bug which he used to reveal how an individual's beliefs can be a help or a hindrance in solving problems. Let us look at Rokeach's explanation of the problem involving Joe Doodlebug.

The Conditions

Joe Doodlebug is a strange sort of imaginary bug. He can and cannot do the following things:

1. He can jump in only four different directions, north, south, east, and west. He cannot jump diagonally (e.g., southeast, northwest, etc.).
2. Once he starts in any direction, that is, north, south, east, or west, he must jump four times in that same direction before he can switch to another direction.
3. He can only jump, not crawl, fly, or walk.
4. He can jump very large distances or very small distances, but not less than one inch per jump.
5. Joe cannot turn around.

The Situation

Joe has been jumping all over the place getting some exercise when his master places a pile of food three feet directly west of him. Joe notices that the pile of food is a little larger than he. As soon as Joe sees all this food he stops dead in his tracks facing north. After all his exercise Joe is very hungry and wants to get the food as quickly as he possibly can. Joe examines the situation and then says, "Darn it, I'll have to jump four times to get the food."

The Problem

Joe Doodlebug was a smart bug and he was dead right in his conclusion. Why do you suppose Joe Doodlebug had to take four jumps, and no more and no less, to reach the food?

Arriving at a Solution

There are three beliefs the subject must first overcome one by one, and three new beliefs which must replace the ones overcome. Then he must somehow integrate these new beliefs into the problem solution.

1. *The facing belief.* In everyday life we have to face the food we are about to eat. But Joe does not have to face the food in order to eat it. He can land on top of it.

2. *The direction belief.* In everyday life we can change direction at will. But Joe is not able to do so because he is forever trapped facing north. Thus, the only way Joe can change direction is by jumping sideways and backwards.

3. *The movement belief.* When we wish to change direction in everyday life there is nothing to stop us from doing so immediately. But Joe's freedom of movement is restricted by the fact that once he moves in a particular direction—north, south, east or west—he has to continue four times in this direction before he can change it. Thus, when Joe stops to survey the situation at the moment his master places the food down three feet west of him, he may or may not necessarily be a free agent. He may have stopped in the middle of a sequence of jumps rather than at the end of a sequence.

Many subjects have difficulty because they assume that Joe is at the end rather than possibly in the middle of a sequence.

The Doodlebug Problem is quite difficult to solve. The solution is as follows: At the moment Joe's master placed the food down, Joe had already jumped once to the east. He therefore has to jump sideways three times more to the east, and once sideways back to the west, landing on top of the food. He can now eat. Simple as it may appear in retrospect, most subjects need help if they are to solve it within a 30- to 45-minute time limit. The reason it is so difficult to solve is that the subject must first overcome not one but three currently held beliefs, and replace them with three new ones. This is the *analytic* phase of the problem. But this is not all. Even if the subject overcomes and replaces all three beliefs with new ones, he still has work to do. He must then organize them together, or integrate them, into a new system. This is the *synthesizing* phase of the problem.*

* In typical research on thinking (Duncker, 1954; Luchins, 1942; Johnson, 1955; Maier, 1930), the obstacle to the problem solution is usually a single belief or set, the overcoming of which is equivalent to the solution. But real-life problems are generally more complicated than this, typically involving the overcoming of multiple rather than single be-

The two processes are depicted graphically below.

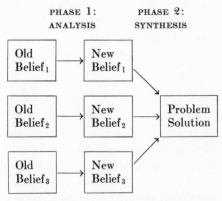

PHASE 1: ANALYSIS	PHASE 2: SYNTHESIS

The analysis phase of the problem is directed toward overcoming old beliefs or sets and replacing them with new ones. Rokeach's results indicated that people considered as either close-minded or open-minded did not differ in the analysis phase. However, those who had a high rigidity score differed in their ability to analyze from those who were considered non-rigid. The rigidity score was determined by answers to such questions as:

"I always put on and take off my clothes in the same order."

"I never miss going to church."

"I usually check more than once to be sure that I have locked a door, put out a light, or something of the sort."

"I often find myself thinking of the same tunes or phrases for days at a time."

"I prefer to stop and think before I act on even trifling matters."

liefs, and involving further their integration into a new system. In other words, real-life problems typically involve both analysis and synthesis.

In the synthesis phase, the new beliefs must somehow be brought together by the same process of integration and organized into a new system, bringing about the solution of the problem. Although closed-minded and open-minded subjects show similar reactions in the analysis phase, they differ in the synthesis phase. People with closed thinking are resistant to a change in the total belief system because they tend to perceive ideas and other people as threatening to their closed systems. The individuals with closed systems would make remarks such as the following:

"Stupid bug! He could get there in one jump."
"There is probably a catch here."
"Let him starve to death."
"What if you don't agree with it?"
"That's crazy!"
"That's irrelevant."

These comments show the manner of thinking done by persons who have preconceived ideas of the way solutions should be arrived at. The rigid thinkers, once they were through the analysis stage, were able to synthesize the results in about the same manner as the non-rigid thinkers.

This research indicates that an individual's personality and his pattern of behavior in attacking problems are motivating and directing forces toward the speed with which he can perceive and integrate new and different ideas. Both the analysis and the synthesis phases of problem solving as well as the composition of each are very important factors that must be seriously considered by anyone who is concerned with the learning process.

THINKING CLEARLY

We have seen that mental flexibility is an integral part of effective learning. However, being able to consider many ideas and choose among different courses of action often puts us at the mercy of our experiences. What may appear to us to be critical and logical thinking may actually be a reflection of our prejudices and beliefs.

Logical Thinking

To solve a problem or make an important decision, it is necessary to use *logic*, which is the science of thinking clearly. This kind of thinking is used in trying to find the reasons behind beliefs and actions, and it is based on evidence.

The solving of problems involves the making of judgments that are actually related to one another and that lead to a final judgment. As we saw in the preceding section, actually there are two functions involved in making a judgment; one is *analysis*, which means a breaking down of a concept into its separate parts, and the other is *synthesis*, which is the forming of new concepts from the available parts and placing them in appropriate relationship with each other.

There are a number of ways to solve problems using logical thinking. Basically, these methods are the same, and they generally follow these five steps:

1. Recognize the problem and define it.

2. Gather the data related specifically to the problem.

3. Evaluate the data and make a tentative solution.

4. Test the solution and determine best action.

5. Keep an open mind for newer or more appropriate information relative to the problem.

Factors That Cause Illogical Thinking In College

There are a number of negative factors that prevent clear thinking and make the solving of classroom and study problems more difficult.

Superstition: A superstition is an irrational fear of the unknown. For instance, some students believe that carrying a lucky coin or charm or sitting in a certain seat in a classroom, or using one special pen or pencil for exams will protect them from bad luck and may even bring good luck. If bad luck does come, the blame will probably be attributed to factors such as the teacher's grading system. Good luck can be credited to the charm the individual has carried or the pencil he has used. Causative factors such as poor study habits may be overlooked, and the relationships or sequential events may be mistaken for the reason that the bad luck happened. Many students find it hard to accept the fact that there is no magic way to get through college. The best "magic" is the ability to think clearly and act intelligently, rather than to trust to luck.

Prejudice: A prejudice is a preconceived opinion. Prejudiced people make up their minds about something or someone before they have any evidence. Prejudices can prevent the use of logic in dealing with problems. An individual who finds that he possesses a number of prejudices should make every effort to get rid of them or he will find it impossible to think logically.

Strong Emotion: A person who has extreme likes and dislikes creates a barrier to clear thinking. It is natural to be angry at injustice or happy over success, but it is necessary to control strong feelings when trying to solve scholastic or personal problems.

Some other blocks to objective and logical thinking habits are:

"All or nothing" thinking, or believing what we want to believe; ("don't confuse me with the facts, my mind is already made up" technique).

Attempting to explain facts under a single hypothesis without considering all the possible alternatives.

Failing to consider all the data or misinterpreting meanings; accepting incomplete or faulty information, such as is furnished by the phrenologist, astrologist, or handwriting "expert." The phrenologist claims that one's mental powers can be indicated by the shape of the skull; the astrologist says that the stars have a powerful influence on human affairs; the handwriting "expert" professes to be able to analyze a person's character and predict his behavior patterns from a small sample of his handwriting. Although handwriting does indicate observable behavior, it is only one motor area that is being observed. A complete character analysis from the way one walks or one's facial expression would be just as ridiculous. All these so-called experts make analyses and predictions on the basis of unproved and incomplete information.

Mistaking relationship for causation; for example, it is a fact that the more money that is spent for liquor, the higher teachers' salaries become. The implication might be that teachers could get higher salaries if more liquor could be consumed. Actually, consumption of liquor and teachers' salaries both rise when economic conditions are good, but one has no bearing on the other.

Trying to impress or being falsely impressed by unnecessary technical terminology; letting words obscure the idea intended or using terms whose meanings are not precise.

Failing to check one's thinking and opinions against established facts.

MEMORY AIDS

Everyone uses some remembering device. The simplest device—tying a string around a finger—is actually creating discomfort or inconvenience which will develop recall of a specific item or activity at a specific time.

It may be easily seen that the string-around-the-finger method does not help to reinforce the thought. The string itself has no relationship to aid of recall in the memory process. For example, the string may be used one time as a reminder to bring home potatoes. Another time, it may mean bring home onions or a can of peas. Actually, these devices are too involved and difficult to use when the material to be remembered is in any way complicated.

The student should be cautioned against the great desire to develop an intricate memory system. Almost everyone feels the need to improve his memory by some kind of system, but the harm comes from trying to put everything into a mnemonic system and memorizing by means of devices. Most people use the little poem, "Thirty days hath September, April, June, and November; All the rest have thirty-one, save February which alone has twenty-eight." This handy little device helps us to remember the number of days in the month without too much strain.

Others may learn to use the first letters of the words in a series to make a sentence. For example, the spectrum may be learned from the name Roy G. Biv (red, orange, yellow, green, blue, indigo, and violet). From this point, students feel they can indiscriminately use such a system with history, biology, zoology, and other subjects by fixating the material to be remembered with a name, word, or sentence. Of course, disaster comes when they are not quite able to make the kind of word that exactly fits the situation, or they are memorizing twice as much material as would be necessary to remember the facts alone.

However, a person is able to remember dates more easily when they are in chronological order, e.g., 1901, 1905, 1921, 1925. Also, one remembers names or ideas arranged in alphabetical order more easily than when in jumbled order, even when there are gaps. For example, if ideas must be remembered for a business course they may be arranged like this:

Banking and credit . . .
Debits for . . .
Money for loan . . .
Trial balance . . .

This arrangement does not distract the person or cause him to learn the key and the idea, but it does make it easier to assimilate.

Some memories are best helped by visual imagery, some by words, and some by kinesthetic or motor-muscle sense. For instance, when one wants to remember some item at a grocery store, one may mentally take various articles from the shelves. Mentally handling the cans, bottles, and other items and noting if they are round, smooth, soft, etc., gives clues that help in bringing an item to the center of attention when desired. Memories are best retained when they are related to concrete experiences and when one *intends* to remember with planned practice to reinforce the original association.

How to Remember People and Names

To remember people, it is necessary to make an association of face, figure, and behavior with the person's name. Developing a good memory process requires accurate visual observation. Remembering names follows the same pattern as other types of learning. After reading the previous material and perhaps a few outside books, your outline of how to associate people with

their names might be similar to the following:

1. Make the name you want to remember have value to you.
   a. Have monetary value.
   b. Contribute to your well-being.
   c. Be of personal interest. (Football tactics, horse race results, etc., are easily remembered because of personal interest.)
   d. Remember that the name must be used when the person is seen again.
2. Get a clear impression.
   a. Hear accurately; listen carefully.
   b. Ask until the name is clear in your mind.
   c. Repeat to yourself.
   d. Write down if possible (use senses of touch and sight).

3. Paint a picture.
   a. Visualize sharply and clearly.
   b. Clarify details such as color and shape.
   c. Note the relationship of parts to whole and whole to parts.
4. Make many associations.
   a. Attach the name to as many familiar things and people as possible.
   b. Remember humorous details.
   c. Connect the name with objects you like.
5. Use the name; repeat it until it is familiar and fixed in your mind.

People and names are forgotten because they were not clearly fixed mentally at the beginning, or because a sincere effort was not made to get the correct information.

THE TEACHING MACHINE

Research conducted with lower animals has shown that the right sequence of stimulus-response activities can help human beings to learn and behave in ways that were not previously thought possible. B. F. Skinner found that he could train white rats or pigeons to engage in complicated behavior by using rewards for successful responses. O. K. Moore used this principle in teaching two-year-old children to read and write.

The teaching machine does the same thing: it presents a stimulus in a direction toward the desired type of behavior or learning situation and then reinforces it, gradually changing the original behavior pattern into a new pattern. In other words, instead of presenting a student with a problem

and waiting until somehow he is able to perceive the answer, the problem is presented in a manner in which any response that would be effective in eventually solving it would be recognized and rewarded.

The core of the process is designing a series of steps, each one small enough for the student to solve. He will then arrive at a solution to the problem through the accumulation of the various steps or fragments of knowledge toward the overall concept.

The machine presents a means of determining whether the student's answer is right or wrong. The enjoyment that comes from being successful tends to make him retain the knowledge.

The student is active when he studies in this way, since (1) he is interacting with the instructor-programmer through the medium of the teaching machine, (2) there is a means of determining the correctness of each response, and (3) he can see that progress is being made. Also the student is permitted to work within the range of time and speed that is related to his own pattern of learning. Programming is of such a nature that the student begins with materials that are familiar to him; then, through a series of questions, he continues to develop new concepts and usages with ever-widening insight into the formulation of definitions, laws, rules, and principles.

The teaching machine provides the student with one question at a time. The technique known as the "Skinner method" enables the student to write out the answer. After the answer has been written, the program answer is presented by the machine for comparison. The other method used, sometimes referred to as the "Pressey technique," is the selection of the correct answer from a group of answers.

Actually, the machine is merely an adjunct to the program. It is the program that contains the intelligence, not the machine. The machine is simply a way of presenting the programmic materials to the student so that he can respond in a "successful" manner. The ideal teaching machine program is one in which the student never makes a mistake; but to have such a program requires constant editing and reworking by the people who are going to use it.

One of the most important advantages of teaching by machine is a pattern of organized answers that can be offered to the student. The material is presented in logical steps. Thus, if the student is not able to answer certain questions, he knows that it is necessary to return to some basic information which he has not learned. The machine will not present concepts and ideas of a higher order until the fundamental ones are understood. The teaching machine may help both teacher and student by emphasizing the importance of teaching and learning by using a logical sequence of ideas.

However, education is more than accumulating knowledge. Much of the interest and enjoyment of obtaining knowledge comes through contacts with the instructor and other students. The manner in which the instructor presents the material and the discussion of concepts as they are interpreted form an integral part of our education.

Man's behavior is influenced by all the knowledge he has accumulated and much of it cannot be interpreted as black or white, right or wrong, or in the specific terms given by a machine.

Undoubtedly, the teaching machine will take over some of the educational process because some things may be more quickly and accurately taught in this way. However, there is little likelihood that it will ever take over the whole process.

HYPNOSIS AND LEARNING

Students are continually trying to find a way of shortcutting the study procedure and are often interested in the value, if any, of hypnosis in learning. Authorities agree that hypnosis can bring about a state of relaxation and can produce a feeling of readiness to learn. However, it is felt that to develop a greater learning capacity than an individual possesses naturally, is impossible.

Recently, a number of newspaper and magazine articles have appeared, telling how hypnosis has been helpful to certain actors in enabling them to memorize material when they are under great stress. The person trying to learn the lines of a play through hypnosis is able to achieve a more concentrated focussing of attention because stress is reduced and outside distractions are minimized.

But learning by rote is not the kind of learning that is most effective in college. Information presented in courses not only has to be memorized, but the various aspects of new concepts must be tied together and then associated with related concepts. Such intense focussing as occurs in hypnosis has the same effect as tunnel vision; for the best understanding of educational material the peripheral ideas must not be excluded.

At the present time, more specific information is needed about the effectiveness of hypnosis in learning before it can be substituted for the study procedures outlined in other chapters.

COMPREHENSION AND LEARNING

The discussion in this chapter has shown us that the process of learning is based on the individual's response to the stimulus. The effect of the material to be studied on the sensory mechanism and the selection and rejection which comes from past experiences combine to bring about comprehension and learning.

See-think-integrate describes the fundamental process of study and learning; the student must rely upon himself to bring about improvement in each of these three areas. Therefore, a more detailed analysis is presented here so that you can see the ways in which thinking and integration can result in comprehension.

1. To get the overall impression of a selection or a paragraph and to grasp the main thought, try to:
   a. Know the particular meaning of words in context.
   b. Understand the thought organization—relationships between sentences or parts of a paragraph, between paragraphs, between ideas.
   c. Differentiate between the significant and the minor or unimportant points.
   d. Remember significant details by:
      (1) Giving proper emphasis to key words.
      (2) Obtaining the exact understanding needed to carry out instructions.
      (3) Synthesizing all elements.
      (4) Having adequate vocabularies, both general and technical.
   e. Concentrate on reading for deeper meaning.
   f. Maintain the thought that you will want to reproduce what has been read.
   g. Develop the habit of rapid, comprehensive reading in order to follow the author's pattern of thought; keep several words and phrases in mind at one time—each is intended to convey meaning as well as to modify, thus producing the author's ideas.
   h. Develop flexibility in thinking; realize that concepts are not wholly right or wrong, pure black or pure white, but some shade of grey.

2. To discover the author's purpose and understand his point of view, make an effort to:
   a. Appreciate the author's art and feel an emotion or a mood.
   b. Evaluate the information presented—think beyond it, judge its validity and completeness, make inferences from it.
   c. Relate what is being read to what is already known or has been read.
   d. Discriminate between fact and opinion in the material read.
   e. Fit together the ideas in an integrated whole.
3. To suit course work to intelligence level, you should:
   a. Know your chances of success from aptitude and intelligence tests and choose courses accordingly.
   b. Use minor successes and failures to predict chances of major success—e.g., two failures in beginning algebra would be an indication of probable lack of engineering ability.
4. To develop interest in subject matter, understand that:
   a. An increase in knowledge of a subject eventually brings about greater interest in it.
   b. Each person's feelings about things depends upon his particular heredity, training, experiences, and personal interests.
   c. Competing with yourself helps develop interest; see how many pages you can read and understand in two fifteen-minute periods, or how long it takes to read several groups of ten pages; strive to make each reading better than the last—more speed and comprehension.
5. To utilize background knowledge, realize:
   a. A foundation is necessary for skill—a foreign language may be difficult because of insufficient knowledge of English grammar; proficiency in college math requires skill in arithmetic.
   b. There is interrelationship between causes.
   c. What you read should be related to some of your aims and purposes; look for personal or social implications—become involved with the ideas.
   d. No one knows all about everything, but it is good to have as many related facts as possible at your disposal. Try not to draw inferences without adequate data.
6. To develop ability to control and direct attention, learn to:
   a. Narrow the field of attention so the subject matter being studied appears in greater focus.
   b. Start studying with vigor as though interested in the assignment; often this will lead to actually becoming interested.
   c. Use discrimination in selecting whatever is significant to the subject studied.
   d. Develop a habit of sustained attention.
   e. Summarize to yourself the

thought of each main section read.

f. Develop a habit of active reaction to what you read.

g. Anticipate the problems that are to come; begin synthesis early.

7. To develop definite, positive study habits, try to:

a. Study specific subjects at regular times and places; taking advantage of the habit-forming tendency makes attention easier to sustain.

b. Learn to disregard distractions by persisting in study in spite of them.

c. Have your own petty rewards and penalty system; deny yourself a snack or the reading of an interesting letter until you finish a certain portion of your studying.

d. Realize that developing good study habits requires diligent effort.

Reference

1. Milton Rokeach, *The Open and Closed Mind,* Basic Books, New York, 1960.

Test Yourself on Chapter 10

Define these terms
 Superstition
 Rigid thinking
 An open mind
 Synthesis
 Logic
 Prejudice
 Analysis

Complete these sentences:
1. Dates are more easily remembered when ⸻⸻.
2. Hypnosis can be helpful in some kinds of learning because ⸻⸻ ⸻⸻.
3. The teaching machine utilizes this principle: ⸻⸻.
4. To remember people, one must associate ⸻, ⸻, and ⸻ with ⸻.
5. The fundamental process of study and learning is ⸻⸻ ⸻⸻.
6. The five general steps in problem solving are:
  (1)
  (2)
  (3)
  (4)
  (5)

11
STUDYING SPECIFICS

STUDYING MATHEMATICS

Understanding Math Fundamentals

The sciences have been built on a basis of mathematical knowledge. The science student should enjoy working with numbers and be able to perform the fundamental processes such as addition, subtraction, multiplication, and division with accuracy and speed. He should know some operations without having to "stop and think" about them.

All the basic principles of arithmetic are important, and especially in college, they must be handled with ease. Fractions in particular are necessary in a number of operations. Remember these basic rules:

Adding fractions.

1. Denominators must be the same.
2. The lowest or smallest number

The author wishes to thank Miss Clela Hammond and other members of the Mathematics Department of El Camino College for assistance in this subject area.

that can be divided by all numbers in the denominator should be used.

3. Make fractions equivalent, using a common denominator.

4. AFTER the above steps have been done, ADD.

Example:

$$\frac{1}{2} + \frac{1}{3} + \frac{1}{4} = \frac{6}{12} + \frac{4}{12} + \frac{3}{12}$$
$$= \frac{13}{12} = 1\frac{1}{12}$$

Hint: Try the two largest numbers multiplied together and see if the others can be divided into it. If this does not produce a common denominator for the remaining numbers, multiply by the largest number that will not go in. Then try the other fractions to see if a common denominator has been obtained.

Subtracting fractions. Follow the same procedure as above, but subtract.

Multiplying fractions. Multiply numerators and denominators together. *Example:*

$$\frac{2}{3} \times \frac{3}{4} = \frac{6}{12}$$

$$\frac{2}{5} \times \frac{3}{5} = \frac{6}{25}$$

$$2 \times \frac{2}{3} = \frac{4}{3} = 1\frac{1}{3}$$

Dividing fractions. Invert and then multiply. *Examples:*

$$\frac{2}{3} \div \frac{3}{4} = \frac{2}{3} \times \frac{4}{3} = \frac{8}{9}$$

$$\frac{2}{7} \div \frac{1}{5} = \frac{2}{7} \times \frac{5}{1} = \frac{10}{7} = 1\frac{3}{7}$$

Proportions. These are a special type of fraction in which the two parts are equal. For example, in a proportion, $\frac{3}{4} = \frac{6}{8}$ is generally written: $3:4::6:8$; it is read as: 3 is to 4 as 6 is to 8. The problem presents a condition which requires the student to solve for one of the numbers when the other three are given. In this example, we will solve for X:

$$3 \quad : \quad 4 \quad :: \quad 6 \qquad X$$

(extreme) (mean) (mean) (extreme)

Multiply *means* and *extremes:*

$$3X = 24$$

$$X = 8$$

The problem is solved in the same way whether the missing number is a mean or an extreme.

If you have trouble with any of the basic processes of arithmetic which should have been mastered in high school, you should review them until you can easily work the problems involved. Use a high school math text or get a special book on remedial math and practice the problems every day.

How to Study Mathematics

There are many ways of studying mathematics. The following method is presented in some detail because it represents a system that has been proven effective, expecially with students having trouble learning algebra.

This method consists of well-known psychological principles put together in a simple, practical system to help students learn more rapidly and effectively. The procedures [1] were tested on freshmen and sophomores who were beginning algebra students.

The Bartlett Time-Centered Study Habit Technique

STEP 1. Have on hand a pencil, paper, and a timer.

STEP 2. Survey rapidly the material to be covered in the lesson.

STEP 3. Choose a portion of the text that you are certain you can cover in 2, 3, or 4 minutes. Set the timer.

STEP 4. Rapidly read over the portion allocated. Then read the first sentence and immediately look away from the text and recite that idea in your own words. Check your work by reading it again. Then read the second sentence, look away, and recite. Check your work. Continue through the allocated portion. Then look away and recite the entire portion and decide how it will look on the paper. When the timer indicates, close the book and write the portion on the paper in your own words. Check the accuracy of your work with the book open.

STEP 5. Give yourself a grade on your work. Consider your grade and the time used on the last portion, allocate a new part and a new time.

STEP 6. Repeat STEP 4, followed by STEP 5.

STEP 7. When you have finished the theory in the text and have made a satisfactory grade on each portion, start on the problems by working the first one on paper; as soon as you have checked the answer, work another.

STEP 8. As soon as the lesson is completed, look over the entire textbook assignment (by looking at the book for clues only) and practice the recitation of the lesson. While this is being done, a portion of the material might prove difficult to recall, and this is the portion that the teacher should be asked to explain. Your ability to continue this method throughout the text depends on your clear understanding of each lesson. Any part of the lesson that is not clear must be cleared up in class.

The Bartlett method is one that brings into focus many of the accepted practices suggested in this book and others. The outstanding element is the use of a timer for studying; this is an integral part of the process. The utilization of a specific period of time is fundamental to developing efficiency and eliminating distracting elements.

The student using this method may be compared to an efficiency expert timing himself with a stopwatch to see that a unit of work is performed during the allocated period. In industry, a time study man determines how many units of production are possible in a specific length of time. In the Bartlett method of study, the timer is used to determine production rate and also production waste.

Step 2 is similar to recommendations of most of the recognized authorities in the field of study: to quickly scan the required work in order to form an overall picture and determine what to study in the time allotted.

The point of departure from most of the usual study methods is in the third step. It was found that having the student set the goal for himself and decide how much time to allow was the best way to adapt this system to the needs of the individual.

The manner in which the actual studying is done (Step 4) prevents any superficial approach to the study situation. This is because the student must become involved in the material. The procedure used is different from taking notes with the book open, and it is also different from oral recitation. The student, by writing down what he has studied in his own words, is using muscle sense to reinforce the thought process. This can be of great help during essay tests. If he is asked questions on this material, he will remember and be able to write about it more easily because of the way in which he has already reproduced it during study. Also, being able to write in his own words the essence of what he has read proves to the student that he really understands what he is studying.

In Step 5, the student compares what he has written with the material in the text and gives himself a grade. The purpose of the grade is to help determine the amount of material and the length of time to allocate for the next portion. If the assigned portion has been completely learned, the student may assume he has allowed the length of time best suited to his individual needs. If not enough of the material has been learned, more time should be allowed for the learning process.

The method involves the self-competitive type of learning in which the pressure comes from trying to learn the material as fast as possible. A certain amount of satisfaction is derived from knowing at this point that the text matter learned has a specific grade equivalent. The student realizes that if he were given a test on the material he has studied in this way, he would probably make this same grade.

This technique of reading, writing, and checking is continued until the entire assignment has been studied. When the worked-out examples have been mastered, then it is time to start the exercises at the end of the chapter; these involve the actual application of the theory that has been learned. It is suggested that the answer to each problem be checked so the correct result can reinforce the feelings of satisfaction.

In Step 8, Bartlett emphasizes the need for thorough understanding of each assignment. After the completion of the lesson, the entire assignment should be recited. If any part of the material is hard to recall, the teacher should be asked to explain it.

Word Problems in Mathematics and Science

The key to success in studying verbal mathematical problems is *accuracy*. In working word problems, the most important point to emphasize is understanding just what the problem tells you. You must read it carefully and know exactly what is asked for so that a solution can be reached in the proper manner. In mathematics, an answer that is "almost" right is unacceptable. The laws of mathematics are unchangeable, even though students often try to prove the answers are "more correct" than the correct ones.

A student must understand the words and symbols involved in the problem and know their proper spelling and usage so that his answer will be accurate. Also, readable writing is especially important in working word problems. The careless student making an χ may interpret it as an x, y, or v as he recopies the letter.

REMEMBER: In *mathematics, letters* are used as symbols for *numbers*.

One must not cross out letters *indiscriminately* and become a victim of "cancel fever." Even the farmer who had 44 acres of squash to fence with 144 posts could not solve the problem by writing:

$$\frac{\text{44 acres of squash}}{\text{144 square fence posts}} = \frac{\text{ash}}{\text{1 spent}}$$

and conclude that one farmer spent his money for ash posts. Then why this?

$$\frac{\text{tan 44}}{\text{sin 4}} \quad \text{or}$$

$$\frac{8a + b}{8} \neq a + b \quad \text{or}$$

$$\frac{3d + b}{d} \neq 3 + b$$

Here = means equal; ≠ means not equal.

Learn when to use the proper symbol.
Don't: $\sqrt{X} = 4 = X = 16$
Do: $\sqrt{X} = 4; \quad X = 16$

Observe the = sign and treat each side equally. If the right side is decreased by a, the left side is decreased by the same amount a:

$$X + a = b$$

(Take away or subtract a):

$$-a = -a$$
$$X = b - a$$

If the right side is divided by a number, so is the left side:

$$ax = b$$

$$\frac{ax}{a} = \frac{b}{a}$$

$$x = \frac{b}{a}$$

If one side is multiplied by a number, the other side is multiplied by the same number:

$$\frac{Y}{2}(a + b) = 6 \quad \text{NOT}$$

$$Y(a + b) = 3$$

MULTIPLY BOTH SIDES BY 2:

$$Y(a + b) = 12$$

Don't drop parts of an equation. Keep the same meaning and value.

$3(x + 4) = 24$ is NOT $3x + 4 = 24$

$\sqrt{a + b}$ is NOT $\sqrt{a} + \sqrt{b}$

When in doubt, try numbers like

$$a = 4 \qquad b = 5$$

$\log(a + b)$ is NOT $\log a + \log b$

$\sin(a + b)$ is NOT $\sin a + \sin b$

Don't drop numbers below the line.
The denominator indicates value as
well as the numerator:

$$\frac{X}{4} + \frac{2X}{4} \neq 3X$$

Try $$X = 1$$

$$\frac{1}{4} + \frac{2}{4} = \frac{3}{4}$$

When the problem is more complicated, the same rule applies:

$$X + \frac{2 - X}{4} = \frac{4X + 2 - X}{4}$$

Note:

$$\frac{a + b}{c} = \frac{a}{c} + \frac{b}{c}$$

Try

$$a = 1 \qquad b = 2 \qquad c = 3$$

$$\frac{1 + 2}{3} = 1; \qquad \frac{1}{3} + \frac{2}{3} = 1$$

BUT:

$$\frac{c}{a + b} \neq \frac{c}{a} + \frac{c}{b}$$

$$\frac{3}{1 + 2} \neq \frac{3}{1} + \frac{3}{2}$$

Watch exponents:

$$a^x \cdot a^y = a^{x+y}$$

$$a^n \cdot b^n = (ab)^n$$

$$3^x \cdot 9^y = 3^x \cdot 3^{2y}$$

Remember letters are symbols for
special numbers. You are held ac-
countable for their behavior at all
times. Use care, consideration, and
understanding.

Converting terms. One of the biggest difficulties that students have in
handling word problems is understanding the value words and converting from one term to another, still
keeping the same value. Many of the
transitions made in problem equations
are based on the assumption that any
number may be multiplied by one or a
fraction representing one without
changing its value. For example:

$$10 \times 1 = 10$$

$$10 \times \frac{2}{2} = \frac{20}{2} = 10$$

$$10 \times \frac{10}{10} = \frac{100}{10} = 10$$

This principle is put into practice in
the following problem:

If an auto is traveling at 75 miles an
hour, how many feet will it travel in
a second?

If we write 75 miles/1 hour and realize that we want to get feet/1 second,
then the relationship between words is
recognized. Stated differently, we
want to change miles to feet and hours
to seconds. So:

$$\frac{75 \text{ mi}}{1 \text{ hr}} \cdot \frac{5280 \text{ ft}}{1 \text{ mi}}$$

We put the unit miles on the bottom
because we can cancel the miles out.
(Notice what can be cancelled and how
it is done. The same unit is *above* the
line as *below* before we can cancel):

$$\frac{75 \text{ \cancel{mi}}}{1 \text{ hr}} \cdot \frac{5280 \text{ ft}}{1 \text{ \cancel{mi}}}$$

Now we have feet per hour:

$$\frac{75}{1 \text{ hr}} \cdot \frac{5280 \text{ ft}}{1} \cdot \frac{1 \text{ hr}}{60 \text{ min}}$$

We now cancel hours out and have feet per minute:

$$\frac{75}{1 \cancel{\text{ hr}}} \cdot \frac{5280 \text{ ft}}{1} \cdot \frac{1 \cancel{\text{ hr}}}{60 \text{ min}} \cdot \frac{1 \text{ min}}{60 \text{ sec}}$$

Next, we cancel minutes out and have feet per second:

$$\frac{75}{1} \cdot \frac{5280 \text{ ft}}{1} \cdot \frac{1}{60} \cdot \frac{1}{60 \text{ sec}}$$

$$75 \times 5280 \text{ ft} \div 60 \times 60 \text{ sec}$$

$$\frac{396000 \text{ ft}}{3600 \text{ sec}} \quad \text{or:} \quad \frac{110 \text{ ft}}{1 \text{ sec}}$$

or: 110 ft per sec

State the problem two ways. Many times, the solution to a problem can be seen when it is stated in *two ways*. For example:

The sum of three consecutive even numbers is 24. What are the numbers?

X is the first even number

$X + 2$ is the second even number

$X + 4$ is the third even number

The problem asks for the sum so add and get the sum:

$$3X + 6 = \text{sum}$$

But the problem gave 24 as the sum:

$$24 = \text{sum}$$

The problem is stated two ways: in terms of X and in terms of 24. Now an equation can be made:

$$3X + 6 = 24$$

Number versus value. The student should realize the differences between the words of *number* and those of *value*. For example:

A student has $1.12 made up of an equal number of pennies, nickels, and dimes. How many of each kind does he have?

X number of pennies @ value of 1¢ each or 0.01X, value of pennies

X number of nickels @ value of 5¢ each or 0.05X, value of nickels

X number of dimes @ value of 10¢ each or 0.10X, value of dimes

Now we can express the total value as:

$$0.01X + 0.05X + 0.10X = \text{total value}$$

The second way of expressing the value was as cited in the problem:

$$\$1.12 = \text{total value}$$

When the facts are expressed in two ways they are equal to each other; this makes the equation:

$$0.01X + 0.05X + 0.10X = \$1.12 \quad \text{or}$$
$$0.16X = \$1.12$$

Number		*Value*
$X = 7$ pennies have the value of		0.07
$X = 7$ nickels " " " "		0.35
$X = 7$ dimes " " " "		0.70

A total value of $1.12

Draw a picture. When you find yourself puzzled by a problem and unable to reach a solution, try to draw a picture from the information given. This may help you to understand the conditions stated in the problem. For example:

A train, traveling at a constant speed

of 75 miles an hour, leaves Chicago for New York (900 miles from Chicago) at 7:00 A.M. Another train, traveling at 50 miles an hour, leaves New York for Chicago. When these two trains meet, which one will be closer to Chicago?

This problem becomes simple when you draw a picture.

drill. Most teachers feel that language students should emphasize relearning and review, so that the material becomes as familiar as the multiplication tables.

Many foreign-language teachers agree that if a student has a good memory for detail and can hear and reproduce sounds accurately, he will not have

STUDYING A FOREIGN LANGUAGE

In learning a foreign language, the student should keep in mind these three important concepts:

1. The alphabet should be memorized and the sounds of each letter should be learned.

2. The words must be heard correctly, then repeated aloud, using the same sounds that were heard. The student should constantly strive to perfect his pronunciation.

3. The meaning and interpretation of words must be memorized and used often in sentences, both oral and written, so they will eventually become a part of the student's speaking and thinking.

Understanding and using a foreign language is a skill, like playing the piano, and the only way to perfect this skill is through constant practice and

too much trouble. Also, it is much easier to learn words in a foreign language if one has a good vocabulary in his own language. This enables him to make many associations between similar words in both languages.

Vocabulary

Many language instructors believe that the shadings of meanings of words are actually more important than the vocabulary itself. Because of this, teachers usually emphasize that a vocabulary cannot be learned in one big swoop, but that it is necessary to constantly review both the vocabulary and the context material. In this way, they hope to engender in the student a *feeling* for the language and an understanding of the patterns of expression that are an integral part of effectively learning a language.

Most students find that using cards to memorize a foreign vocabulary is an effective learning method. The word is written on one side of a small card and the translation on the other. This can be very helpful in memorizing the words that were looked up during a reading and translating session. These cards can be kept in a pocket or purse so they may be used for review in spare moments. When a word has been memorized, the card can be removed so that the stack is kept small enough to be handled easily.

Although foreign language vocabulary cards may be purchased ready-made, it is better for the student to make his own. The effort expended in choosing the words, writing them down, and writing the translations will help the learning process.

Idioms

Understanding idioms usually is a difficult part of a foreign language course. Idioms are expressions which are peculiar to a language. They are word combinations which, literally translated often have little or no meaning, but taken as a whole, indicate

something definite. Take, for example, these two Spanish idioms, both based on the same two words:

Idiom
¿Qué hay? = What's the matter?
Hay que (+ infinitive) = One must; it is necessary to.

Literal English Translation
¿Qué?–What?
que —as, than, who, which, that, for.
hay —there is, there are.

Idioms are important because they provide color and authenticity that is missing when a language is spoken with exact textbook correctness. The only way to learn idioms is to memorize them and then use them orally and written in sentences, until they become a natural part of the vocabulary.

Grammar

The rules of grammar must not only be memorized but practiced until the student uses them automatically. It is of small value to memorize lists of nouns and verbs unless their meaning and use is understood. Such memorization can be helpful in certain kinds of examinations, but is of little value in developing understanding and correct usage in sentences.

Cognates

Words which have similar meanings and spelling in several languages are called *cognates*. Spanish, French, and German, for instance, contain a number of words which are very much like their English equivalents. You can probably guess the meanings of these cognates quite easily:

German	French	Spanish
interesse	deux	dificultad
über	comprendre	grande
traum	contre	dirección
todt	intérieur	molestar

Reading and Translating

As a language student advances, he will begin reading paragraphs and short stories. A good way to pick up reading speed and general comprehension is to read through a selection, not looking up unfamiliar words, but depending upon context for meaning. This is where the use of cognates can be very helpful.

However, there are cognate words which once had the same meanings but which have developed different meanings through usage. Therefore, *all* new words should be looked up after a reading session so the meanings are very clear.

Reading for understanding of the whole rather than of individual words is valuable because the student can get the "feel" of the language and the word patterns. But using this technique alone can be hampering if one does not get the full meaning of all the words from the context. Word-for-word translation is necessary when a passage is not clear.

When translating each word in a selection, it is not a good idea to write the meanings between the lines in the textbook. Although this may save time because the words do not have to be looked up again, the student is depriving himself of chances to restudy words of which he is uncertain and fix them in his mind.

Practice and Repetition

The importance of constant practice and repetition in learning a foreign language cannot be overemphasized. If possible, a student should hold conversations with friends who speak the language. Most schools have foreign language clubs that provide excellent opportunities for conversing. Larger cities usually have theaters that feature foreign movies. Foreign language newspapers and magazines are an interesting way to practice reading. Reading aloud and listening to people who speak the language fluently (either in person or on special recordings) will help to perfect pronunciation. Studying a language in different ways helps to prevent monotony and provides chances for valuable practice.

STUDYING CHEMISTRY

In studying chemistry, the complete text assignment should first be read, and an effort should be made to understand the variations of the basic concepts and the way they fit together.

After the entire assignment has been read and studied, the student will find it very helpful to read an outline study guide. This is a paperbacked book that contains a condensed version of the chemistry course.

The chemistry textbook is written with the objective of being accurate and including many details that may be helpful in understanding the main concepts. However, the beginning student may not be able to separate the more important ideas from those that are less important. The study guide covers the essential elements of the course and helps to crystallize ideas. Also, its brevity and conciseness makes it excellent for review.

This method of supplementing the text material gives the student another version of the same concepts, since a different set of words is used. Also, the ideas are expressed more directly and concisely. The basic skeleton of the material stands out, in the same way as a skeleton on an x-ray plate. When the student rereads the textbook, he can add the body.

Since the study guide is not as complete as the textbook, it must be used in conjunction with it. One should never depend on a condensed version of the text to provide all the information needed in a complicated science course.

Another learning aid for chemistry students is this one suggested by an instructor in chemistry. He says: "I give my students a list of words and tell them I will discuss them sometime during the course; I suggest that they try to understand these terms. I find that during lectures they are continually watching for the words; and after-

ward they discuss with each other the definitions and explanations given for them."

It is a fact that most courses are tied in with vocabulary and general understanding of terms, but it is especially true in science courses. It would be a sound learning practice for a student to prepare a list of words that he would like to know more about and then see what the instructor says about them.

STUDYING THE LIFE SCIENCES

In studying life sciences (biology, zoology, botany), it is necessary to have a very good visual memory. These courses require a great deal of memory. This is somewhat different from math, which puts greater emphasis on reasoning. Another extremely important ability, which is perhaps the main factor in studying the life sciences successfully, is seeing the interrelationship among parts, processes, or classes. A person who is able to express this relationship of concepts through diagrams will find this to be a great advantage in learning biological material. In the examples which fol-

Part of Alimentary Canal	Secretion			Enzyme Contained
Buccal cavity	Saliva			Ptyalin
Stomach	Gastric juice			Pepsin
	Rennin—(not an enzyme)—Coagulates soluble milk protein HCl—Acidifies chyme so pepsin has correct pH in which to function. When in duodenum, HCl and fats trigger pancreas to secrete pancreatic juice and liver to secrete bile.			
Small intestine	Intestinal juices	From pancreas		Amylopsin
				Trypsin
				Steapsin
				Erepsin
		From intestine wall		Maltase
				Sucrase
				Lactase
Pancreas	Pancreatic juice			Amylopsin Trypsin Steapsin
Liver	Bile	Bile Salts—Fats emulsified Deposit from bile causes gall stones that may clog bile ducts and cause JAUNDICE (the breakdown products of hemoglobin collect in the skin) Neutralizes duodenum contents (Sodium Bicarbonate)		

Duodenum—Gets juices from pancreas and bile from intestine.
Jejunum—Digestion and begin absorption.
Ileum—Villi increase absorptive area.
Colon—Reabsorption of water.
Rectum—Passage of feces.

-ase -in	Enzyme or hormone
-ose	sugar

SYSTEM *

Acts Upon	Breaks Down Into
Starches	Maltose (double sugar)
Protein	Half-digested proteins
Starches	Maltose (double sugar)
Proteins and partly digested proteins	Further digested proteins
Fats	Fatty acids and glycerol
Partly digested proteins	Amino acids
Maltose	
Sucrose	Single sugars
Lactose	
Secreted into duodenum	

"END PRODUCTS"
Glucose, fructose, and amino acids into capillaries.

Fatty acids and glycerol into lacteals of lymphatic system and this joins blood circulation near heart.

* Adapted from material supplied by Mary Sidey, El Camino College.

DIAGRAM OF DIGESTIVE SYSTEM

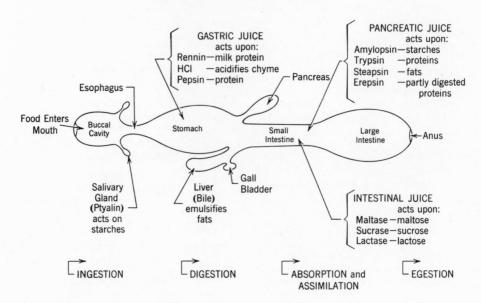

low, note how factual material about digestion has been developed into a chart and then into a simple diagram, which is a help in visualizing the entire process.

Another facet of this interrelationship is understanding in two ways the terms used in these courses: the meaning of the complete word must be known as well as the meanings of the word parts, which are generally derived from the Latin or Greek. As has been shown in an earlier chapter, some of these words can be readily understood by knowing either the prefix or suffix; this can be seen in these examples:

Con-ver gent. Approaching each other or tending toward a common point. (L. *con*, together + *vergo*, incline)

Cu-ta ne-ous. Pertaining to the skin. (L. *cutis*, skin)

In-teg u-ment. An outer covering, especially the skin of a vertebrate and its derivatives. (L. *intego*, to cover)

Sap ro-phyte. An organism that lives upon `dead organic matter. (Gr. *sapros*, rotten + *phyton*, plant)

Tet ra-pod. A vertebrate, typically, with 4 limbs—the amphibians, reptiles, birds and mammals. (Gr. *tetra*, four + *pous*, foot)

Ven tral. Toward the lower side or belly; away from the back. Opposite to the dorsal. (L. *venter*, belly)

Ves sel. A tubular structure that conveys fluid, especially blood or lymph. (L. *vascellum*, diminutive of *vas*, vase)

Vi ta-min. An organic substance that is an essential food factor needed in minute amounts for normal growth and function. (L. *vita*, life + *amin*, a chemical radical)

Another suggestion that is very important in studying the life sciences is to redraw text illustrations instead of just studying them. Then, if a diagram is called for on a test or a reference is made during a class discussion, it will be easier to reproduce or associate material.

Science courses are not easy for most students. It should be realized that a constant, concentrated effort is a requirement for success in the sciences. This is what one zoology instructor tells her beginning students; it could apply to any science course:

The course is divided into lecture and laboratory sections, but do NOT imagine that the laboratory and lecture are separate. They may be held at different hours, but that is just because they demand a different approach. *The lecture and laboratory supplement each other.*

Both in lecture and in laboratory there is too much material to be spelled out word by word, and in many cases there is no need to report upon material because it is quicker for a student to read it on his own. The required texts and lab manuals are provided for this specific purpose. *Assignment by assignment* you must read the text, reread it, and *make your own sheet of notes* on it. If this is a chore you are probably in the wrong course: all academic work needs this approach.

Unless you are a genius, you produce according to the well-known formula: 10% inspiration and 90% perspiration. The "inspiration" you possess may not be open to change, but you *can* do something about the "perspiration."

Keep a record of your own grades, and if you consistently receive D or F, don't hope for the best. But in the light of all your personal factors, re-evaluate your program before you have adversely affected your record. If you find you lack the time, persistence or ability, ask the Instructor if he thinks you would be wise to withdraw, and if he agrees, *do so officially.*

STUDYING ECONOMICS

Economics is the social science which is concerned with the production, distribution, and consumption of services and goods, as well as with the material aspects of living. Because of the many areas included in this science, it is to be expected that the student of economics is required to understand words that carry wide connotations. This is also true of related subjects such as law and political science, as well as some subjects in the business field.

However, studying economics involves not only the understanding of individual words, but also the interrelationship of words and their contribution to whole concepts. Once a concept is developed, it contains a number of words, each of which has a specific meaning in itself; but, at the same time, it has a directional or limiting effect upon the other words with which it is associated. Often the concept becomes part of a larger concept which may combine with others to form a still larger concept; this is called a "series."

Since much of the study of economics is the memorization of terms and principles, the interpretation of key words is important. It is useless to memorize words and laws without understanding the principles from which they have evolved. Because of the multiplicity of associations, it can be seen that to read the material once is centainly not enough to understand all the interrelated ideas.

As an example, let us look at a definition such as this one of diminishing utilities which may be expressed something like this: *in the consumption of a series of identical units at a given point of time, the satisfaction derived from each succeeding unit has less effect than the preceding unit.* Here we find words that must be understood and then interrelated. Such words as "consumption" and "series" are related to a point of time and to decreasing satisfaction. These are the key ideas. The main idea might be thought of as "decreasing satisfaction"; the others are actually related conditions under which the decreasing satisfaction takes place. The given point of time as well as the series of identical units are interrelated and must be understood in relation to particular conditions to form the concept.

Many economic and legal principles are built upon previously established rules, regulations, and limitations. If the basic concepts are not understood, then there is no basis upon which to build and connect additional and related material; therefore, it is necessary for each lesson to be learned before the next lesson is begun. A student trying to skip a part of an assignment is hampering himself because he will lack blocks of knowledge with which to build when he is presented with a problem which requires them.

GENERAL IDEAS ON STUDY

The author asked a number of deans and counselors in several colleges what study hints and general advice they considered most valuable in helping students. A few of their answers are given here.

A dean of a large school believes that many students have the idea that their instructors are out to "get them." He finds they profit more from their studies when they overcome this feeling. He tells such students that they should realize that instructors are "for" them and want to help them learn.

Another dean tries to help confused students by suggesting that they evaluate their situation and ask themselves, "What do I want to accomplish? What should I do to reach my goal?" He tries to help students to think in positive terms of reaching their goals.

A third dean tells students who have either personal or scholastic problems, "No one can tell you what would help you most in solving your problem. Get *all* the information you can about ways of solving it, but *you* must make the final decision."

A counselor for English students says: "Some students believe they can't express themselves well in writing, but they have ideas that would make good compositions or even stories. I suggest to them that they put their ideas on cards and write about them at night for fifteen minutes. By thinking through their ideas and actually developing them on paper, they may become fluent writers."

Another counselor suggests that it is often profitable to compare notes after class with another student. This procedure permits value judgments to take place. One student may get something from the lecture the other didn't or may have taken down points the other thought unimportant. He may then decide that perhaps it *is* important and worth considering since his friend thought so.

An advisor for accounting students says, "When I was an instructor I generally tried to give examples of the material I covered. Then I gave my students different problems to see if they understood what had been discussed. This enabled the student to see what part of the work he was not getting, and he could spend more time reviewing what he did not know. One important point I stress is: *Do not let work that is not understood pile up.* Often a lecture or class discussion is based on material which the instructor assumes has been learned."

Comment: Instructors in many different subjects often use the technique of: (1) explanation, (2) solving of some representative problems, and (3) requiring the student to test himself. *Be sure you understand how to work the problems for each assignment.*

Reference

1. William H. Bartlett, El Camino College, *Time-Centered Study Habit Technique.* Unpublished Master's Thesis, University of California at Los Angeles, 1959.

Techniques for Studying Specific Subjects

Perhaps you are not taking any of the subjects discussed in this chapter. Have you developed some successful techniques for study in other courses? You may have worked out an excellent method for memo-rizing art principles or data in an astronomy course, for instance.

Use this space to jot down your personal study methods. Compare them with those of some of your classmates. You may be able to exchange ideas that will be more helpful than you realize.

SUBJECT   TECHNIQUE

12

EDUCATIONAL AND VOCATIONAL GOALS

FINDING A KEY

There are many vocations and occupations from which you may choose your life's work. Each of these occupations is different in some respect from the others and requires certain abilities. If an individual is to be well adjusted, he must fit the requirements of the job just as a key fits the proper tumblers in a lock. When the peaks and valleys meet a matching pattern, the future can be unlocked, and success is assured.

Just as it is not necessary for a key to have high peaks throughout in order to fit a specific lock or occupation, certain disabilities will not necessarily prevent a person from entering an occupation. Some jobs require ability in a particular area—perhaps mechanical facility or skill in the use of fingers, or skill in the use of eyes or ears—but require a small amount of what we consider "abstract" intelligence.

It is up to each individual to evaluate his own peaks and valleys and match these peaks with the requirements of a specific job.

A REALISTIC OUTLOOK

Many students seem to possess tunnel vision and see only the goal they desire without considering the hard work necessary to reach it. They imagine themselves sitting behind a large desk giving orders which are carried out with pomp and ceremony. Their feelings of self importance are bolstered by these elaborate daydreams. But a tremendous amount of work must be done before a student with an armload of books becomes an executive with papers and telephones on his desk.

EDUCATION AND GOAL SELECTION

Many of the occupations a person may wish to enter require additional education. The student is faced with the problem of determining how education is going to help him meet the requirements of the vocation he would like to enter. He must also consider whether he is going to be able to adjust financially, socially, and in all other respects to making this allocation of time and energy.

It has been fairly well established that a college education will increase the earning power of the individual. However, not all courses have the same value from the standpoint of advancing the person vocationally, culturally, or financially, because of the amount of study or time expended on them (see Figure 1).[1] A course like typing may result in a great amount of vocational gain but very little cultural gain, whereas another course such as literature may

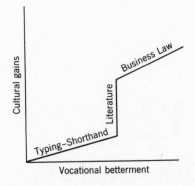

Figure 2

promote a great amount of gain culturally but very little monetary advancement or vocational betterment. A business law course may have some cultural value and also have a vocational use. A course in typing may be followed by a course in shorthand, which would increase the vector in a specific direction toward business proficiency. This may also increase the student's cultural status because of advancement in the hierarchy of the business world. Figure 2 shows how these forces accumulate in the direction of the goal.

The student must determine the aim of his education and select those subjects that will permit him to reach his goal. His choice of courses should broaden his cultural background as well as improve his ability to sell his education to an employer. Taking too many courses of cultural nature would not permit the student to sell himself advantageously, because the business world requires training that enables an individual to utilize specific skills in the process of manufacturing or development. On the other hand, too many courses of the vocational type will limit the person socially; he will not enjoy as

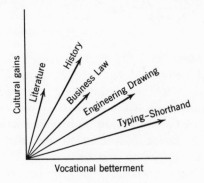

Figure 1

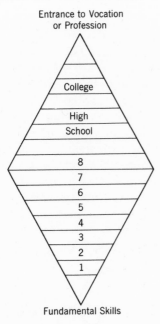

Figure 3

eighth grade the broadening of knowledge and the observation of the environment is emphasized. At that time, there is a turning point in the general direction of the goal or vocational selection in life. The senior in high school or the freshman in college finds it necessary to think seriously of the apex, or the point of entering the workaday world and selecting and pursuing a vocation.

THE WELL-BALANCED COURSE OF STUDY

Students should understand the organization pattern of colleges in order to plan a well-balanced program. In Figure 4, we find that the lower division is divided into state requirements, specific school requirements, major course requirements, and supporting course requirements. For example, the major course might be chemistry, and supporting courses mathematics and physics. In the later years, or upper division, the student will take electives that seem to fit his specific needs. In this division, there is greater emphasis on major courses and supplements to the major courses and on electives. Therefore, it is desirable for the student to take the

full a life as could be attained through a broader knowledge of man's environment. This kind of knowledge can satisfy the esthetic as well as the physical needs of the individual. Many work situations require a person not only to understand the technical aspect of the job but have cultural appreciation as well in order to advance in the vocational hierarchy.

In our educational system (see Figure 3), we find that until about the

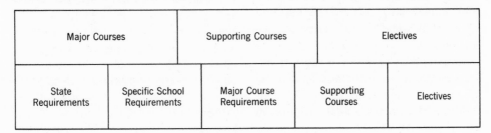

Figure 4

lower-division requirements and get them out of the way during the first years; they are the basic steps toward the wider selection of major courses during the final years of college.

Too many times, students are very anxious to build the educational super-structure without an adequate foundation. The following diagram illustrates this need for stability in the educational program. Two floating corks are shown: the first one, A, has a large mass beneath the surface of the water; the second one, B, has only a small amount of area below the surface. Both may float in that position if there is no turbulence or if there is pressure placed in the exact center. However, if the pressure is placed off-center or if there is a slight amount of turbulence in the water, it is likely that B will cap-size. Regardless of how elaborate the superstructure, it is the large keel on the boat that gives it the stability when the going gets rough.

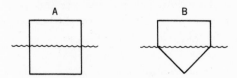

This illustration could be applied to the stresses and strains of life or a vocation. Unless we have an adequate educational and cultural background with established habit patterns, we may become upset and have difficulty maintaining balance. We must therefore carefully evaluate our goals, and develop an adequate foundation for handling the situations that will arise in our chosen vocation.

Too often, students feel that the courses they are required to take in the humanities or the arts are of no practical value. They fail to see that those individuals who are making the greatest strides in business and industry are not necessarily the ones who are technically proficient. They are able to talk with people who know something besides pi r squared (πr^2) or the law of supply and demand. As occupations and industries change and new opportunities arise, the person with the varied, integrated background who is able to adapt to new situations may be the one most wanted.

PROBLEMS IN VOCATIONAL SELECTION

There are often many problems involved in the selection of a vocation. The student wants to be sure that when he leaves the protection of home he is going to be able to provide a suitable economic life for himself. Vocational selection problems are enormous because so many unrealistic concepts are formed through movies, stories, and the values that are placed upon certain occupations because of the monetary reward.

Many times a person will want to go into a specific vocation in which the job opportunities are rather limited. He may have all the characteristics necessary for the job but may find that there are only a few very highly skilled people wanted in this particular type of work. This is particularly true in such vocations as music, which require a considerable amount of training and ability. The person seeking employment in this field may have the ability to do an acceptable job, but the opportunities for making a consistently adequate income from the vocation of music are limited. There are musicians in bands who make very substantial salaries, and there are some teachers of music who also make a fairly good living, but there are not many positions of this kind.

Also, it is necessary for an individual to realize that if he is going into the entertainment field he will not be able to have the same kind of home life as the average person; when he has to work, other people are playing, and when he has time available for recreation, others are working. The problem of working hours may make certain occupations acceptable or not acceptable to a person planning to enter a specific vocation.

This leads to another consideration—the remunerative possibilities of a job. A person may be willing to accept a nominal salary for doing work from which he feels he is learning, but he may not be able to do so because he needs money to support himself and his dependents. This means that although he has enough ability for and interest in a certain vocation, it may be necessary to utilize these qualities in doing work from which he will receive adequate pay and lesser amount of training.

It has been found that if a person is working below capacity—that is, if he has more ability than is required on the job—he may have a tendency to become discontented because of the lack of challenge. The opposite is also true. A person may not have adequate ability to do the job. Hence, the job will require more from him than he is able to produce, and this leads to frustration. He will feel continually harassed not only in his work but in his contacts with others; his home life may also be disrupted because he is not able to satisfactorily meet the challenge of the job. Therefore, personal ability must be evaluated in terms of the job requirements. However, it must be remembered that no job is going to offer just the right amount of challenge at all times to prevent boredom and the right amount of successful attainment to prevent frustration.

Analyzing Interests and Abilities

Some persons have so many interests that they may be confused in selecting a vocation. However, a variety of interests does not necessarily have to limit the progress toward one's vocational goal. Analyzing certain traits and abilities can help in making a decision. Many jobs require certain types of personalities for success. If a person does not have these character traits, he will be hampered from the beginning. It may be possible for him to change his personality if he should really want to, but an evaluation must first be made to determine the type of person he is at the present time. The following are some of the more important areas that should be analyzed.

Intelligence. Occupational groups tend to have different levels of intelligence. The *Army General Classification Tests* [2] disclosed that some occupations require more intelligence than others. At the top of the list was the accountant; in fifth place, the chemical engineering student; in tenth place, the pharmacist; in twentieth place, the radio repair man; in seventieth place, the electrical instrument man; in eightieth place, the combination welder; in ninetieth place, the pipe fitter; in one-hundredth place, the tractor driver. It is easy to see how these occupations would require different levels of intellectual ability. There is, however, a range of ability within any occupation.

It has been found that persons with high intelligence are unhappy in routine jobs, but persons with low intelligence like routine jobs and are unhappy in work requiring problem solving and decision making. An interesting experiment along this line was conducted by one of the utility companies during the depression. At that time, the company was able to obtain intellectual people of Ph.D. caliber to do routine and quickly learned jobs. Although these people could do the work,

they became disgusted with the type of activity involved. They were unsettled and were poor production-line workers, for there was considerable competition within this group for any advancement or opportunity to change to a different kind of work. The company found that it was better to hire people with lower intelligence and fit them into this specific type of work. Then, through normal growth and development on the job, these individuals could be promoted. These people liked the company, produced more, were more willing to stay with the company for a longer period of time, and had greater feelings of satisfaction and belonging.

Verbal ability. Another important factor in vocational adjustment is verbal ability. Some positions require a considerable amount of writing, reporting, and speaking. Perhaps, in a broad sense, all jobs require a little salesmanship and the communication of ideas. If a person has this ability, many opportunities are open to him, but being unable to express himself adequately may prevent him from fitting into many positions.

Mathematical ability. Mathematical ability is another factor that the student should consider as he looks toward vocational adjustment. There are many students who like mathematics and have a natural ability for it. There are others who find this area dull and uninteresting and are not able to perform adequately in it no matter how much training they receive. The lack of ability to see things quantitatively and to handle numbers in the abstract is looked down on in this scientific age. However, this is actually nothing to be ashamed of, since people either have this ability or they do not.

Sociability. Social insight enables a person to handle other people better. The sociable person may prefer to have a work environment in which there are others close by. There are individuals who just seem to have natural tact; and, to some, the understanding of people in groups seems to take place without effort. Those who have this ability of working in harmony with others should select their work accordingly. Vocations too will differ in their requirements for persons with social aptitude.

Mechanical ability. Mechanical ability enables people to manipulate objects, put them together, and see what makes them work. There are individuals who dislike a mechanical pump or motor because it is greasy. They prefer not to handle them because they would get their hands dirty. To other individuals, a broken, greasy motor is a challenge and the most aborbing type of problem into which they could possibly put their time and effort. This insight into mechanical mysteries is a rewarding talent to possess in this mechanistic age.

Special talents. The individual with a special talent in a specific field, such as music, art, or literature, may not always earn his living from the full-time utilization of his special talent. However, in many instances he may use this special talent as a part of his full-time work; this will give the person satisfaction and, consequently, will make him a better-adjusted individual.

FINDING THE RIGHT JOB

The student may be somewhat perplexed in trying to wade through the

great number of job classifications that are available. Perhaps a good place to start would be the *Dictionary of Occupational Titles*. In 1927 the British Ministry of Labour published a comprehensive listing of job types, the *Dictionary of Occupations*. The book contained 16,837 definitions and 27,106 terms. In the United States it was widely used and was the forerunner of the 1939 edition of the *Dictionary of Occupational Titles*. This was followed in 1949 by a dictionary that contained 22,028 definitions of jobs and 40,023 job titles. Revisions of the dictionary are constantly being made and are for sale by the Superintendent of Documents, United States Printing Office, Washington, D. C.

The student at this point may feel he is trying to assemble a complex jig saw puzzle, where each part is impor-

tant enough to make a complete picture. A knowledge of the occupation is necessary to develop a pattern and solve the puzzle. With a number of patterns available, the parts, which represent the individual's aptitudes, interests, and abilities with all of the shadings of intensity, must be carefully selected and assembled into the "best fit." The student's selection of an occupation can be determined by information obtained from testing, evaluating, judging, and fitting to points of reference and value as well as the selection of the best information about the job and himself. The hoped for result is the adjusted individual, "a square peg in a square hole." The process, at best, is difficult, and the student should not be above getting the best vocational help available. The school counselor might aid the student with interpretation of test results and make available adequate counseling services.

References

1. Diagrams used from unpublished material in a study made by Gerald Brown, El Camino College, California.
2. *Army General Classification Tests,* Examiner's Manual, First Civilian Edition, Chicago, Science Research Associates.

Self-Evaluation of Vocational Interests

The Vocational Interest Inventory [*] (pages 50–51) is constructed to help you choose a realistic vocational goal by presenting core material in the vocations young men and women are likely to enter. For instance, if a person likes to "work with tools," "knows how a machine is operated," "likes mathematics" and "scientific work," he would be more likely to be a better prospect for the engineering field than one who did not like these things. These are more realistic reasons for choosing engineering than the glamorous considerations of prestige, financial return or hope of adventure. This Inventory is to be used as an aid for crystallizing the student's thinking and throwing light on his possible goals. It is not an intellgence test or a test on school subjects. There are no right or wrong answers.

Evaluating Yourself from the Inventory

1. Look at the first, second, and third choices at the left of the numbers.
2. Examine the items you like *most;* find the items in which you feel you have

[*] Lyle Tussing, *Psychology for Better Living,* John Wiley and Sons, New York, 1959, pp. 427–429.

much ability (check school records when possible).

3. Look at the areas in which you have had experience.

By studying the pattern formed when these work phases are grouped together, these characteristics will begin to suggest themselves. Some of the more masculine traits appear near the beginning of the Inventory, some of the more feminine traits near the end. However, the last five items are generally indicative of college work.

Various items have been shown to be helpful in determining suitability for various vocations. Items 16, 17, 18, 19, and 20 are important in the aviation transportation area. Item 5 is helpful in separating the engineer from the mechanic who works with or on a machine and checks 1, 2, 3, 4, and 7. Skill in 14, 15, 21, 22, 23, and 25 is essential in the sales and business fields. Office work demands ability in 38, 40, 49, 52, and especially 53 and 23. Home Economics involves 55 and variations of 13, 14, 15, 22, 24, 38, 39, 41, and 47. Agricultural pursuits call for 42, 43, and 44, with variations of 44 for veterinarians. Religious pursuits involve variations on 11, 13, 45, 56, and 59. Dentistry includes 1, 2, 8, 9, 22, 40, and 46. Social service is built around 45 and 46. Other specific areas will be evident if the items are given careful consideration. The *Dictionary of Occupational Titles* which was discussed earlier can be very helpful when used with the Inventory.

It is not intended that a student's rating of his abilities should be used as a substitute for his scholastic record or his intellectual rating; instead, it should be used as· additional information. The results of the Invetnory may help the student and his counselors come to a decision on an appropriate career for him.

VOCATIONAL INTEREST INVENTORY

	Lik-ing			Abil-ity in			Expe-rience		
	Much	Some	None	Much	Some	None	Much	Some	None

Name. . . . .
Occupation you prefer to enter. . . . .
Check your degree of liking, ability, and experience in each.
Make X in each section for each item.

... 1. Work with tools (riveter, hand drill, wrenches, etc.)...
... 2. Work which necessitates skill or precision with hands..
... 3. Work with machinery. . . . .
... 4. Work with (underline one) wood, metal, electricity, pipes, cement. . . . .
... 5. Work which necessitates knowing HOW machines operate. . . . .
... 6. Work necessitating physical activity. . . . .
... 7. Work in a factory. . . . .
... 8. Work requiring mixing and testing. . . . .
... 9. Work putting things together; assembling. . . . .
... 10. Work which applies mathematical procedure or statistics
... 11. Work requiring reasoning based on scientific procedures
... 12. Work that has physical danger and risk. . . . .
... 13. Work requiring research and exploration. . . . .
... 14. Work dealing with buying materials. . . . .
... 15. Work dealing with selling materials or services. . . . .
... 16. Work in which cooperation and tact are essential. . . . .
... 17. Work which requires foreseeing consequences and checking same. . . . .
... 18. Work which involves a periodical change of residence
... 19. Work requiring emotional stability under trying conditions. . . . .
... 20. Work requiring punctuality. . . . .
... 21. Work which persuades people. . . . .
... 22. Work demanding a good business sense. . . . .
... 23. Work requiring simple figuring and use of arithmetic..
... 24. Work which involves the entertainment of people. . . . .
... 25. Work requiring the accurate and honest handling of money. . . . .
... 26. Work involving leadership. . . . .
... 27. Work demanding responsibility. . . . .
... 28. Work having many details. . . . .
... 29. Work in which you are directed. . . . .
... 30. Routine work. . . . .
... 31. Work involving sharp or discriminating vision. . . . . . .
... 32. Work involving rapid finger or hand movement. . . . . . .
... 33. Work hitting a spot with an object (rivet in hole, drill on mark). . . . .
... 34. Work where surroundings are noisy. . . . .

	Liking			Ability in			Experience		
	Much	Some	None	Much	Some	None	Much	Some	None
... 35. Work requiring rigid accuracy......................									
... 36. Work requiring considerable speaking.................									
... 37. Work requiring ability to express ideas clearly........									
... 38. Work requiring considerable writing, pen, pencil, or typewriter................									
... 39. Work dealing with creative planning or design........									
... 40. Work in an office........................									
... 41. Work of an artistic nature......................									
... 42. Work out-of-doors........................									
... 43. Work with plants........................									
... 44. Work with animals........................									
... 45. Work involving listening to people and advising them..									
... 46. Work which gives assistance or help to people........									
... 47. Work which instructs and teaches others.............									
... 48. Work exemplifying a high moral character............									
... 49. Work requiring systematic order and neatness........									
... 50. Inside work............................									
... 51. Work requiring neatness of dress at all times.........									
... 52. Work with office machines (typewriter, adding, etc.)..									
... 53. Work requiring spelling, punctuation, correct use of words.........................									
... 54. Work demanding exceptional appearance (beauty, carriage)									
... 55. Work doing cooking, sewing or both.................									
... 56. Work which requires a high scholarship record........									
... 57. Work necessitating listening attentatively and reproducing same........................									
... 58. Work requiring much fast or comprehensive reading...									
... 59. Work requiring technical knowledge.................									
... 60. Work which requires drive and ambition.............									

In the above work situations, indicate your first choice by placing a 1 in front of the item, then indicate your second and third choices in similar fashion.

Analyze an occupational field which interests you

1. Find out such information as:

   Duties in this field.

   The present demand for workers and what the demand is likely to be when you are ready for a job.

   The qualifications one should have for the job in terms of:

   a. Education   d. License or certificate
   b. Experience   e. Personality
   c. Special skills   f. Physical requirements

   Advantages and disadvantages of the job.

   The line of promotion, from beginning positions to positions you should like to attain.

   The salary range.

   Occupations related to this field.

   Where you might look for employment.

   Significant points mentioned by people in the field whom you have interviewed.

   Sources of information about the field; outstanding books or pamphlets on the subject.

2. In Alport-Vernon's Study of Values, six groups (Spanger's types of man) of people's values are listed. How do you react to a mountain in the distance? What type of values are most important to you?

Theoretical type:	"Observe the strata of rock."
Economic type:	"Is there gold in it?"
Aesthetic type:	"The various colors harmonize."
Social type:	"What a fine place for a picnic!"
Political type:	"What about the housing project?"
Religious type:	"It's God's work."

3. Discuss your philosophy of life. What determines your basic attitudes and what will integrate these values with your occupational life?

4. Check any occupation you think you would like to enter. Double check those occupations that are especially appealing.

VOCATIONAL INTERESTS

Outdoor
—Forest Ranger
—Naturalist
—Farmer
—Gardener

Mechanical
—Automobile
    Repairman
—Watchmaker
—Drill Press
    Operator
—Engineer

Scientific
—Doctor
—Chemist
—Nurse
—Engineer
—Radio Repairman
—Aviator
—Dietician

Persuasive (oral
  verbal)
—Actor
—Politician
—Radio Announcer
—Minister
—Salesman
—Store Clerk
—Insurance
    Salesman

Artistic
—Painter
—Sculptor

—Architect
—Dress Designer
—Hairdresser
—Interior Decorator

Literary (written
  verbal)
—Novelist
—Historian
—Teacher
—News Reporter
—Editor
—Drama Critic
—Book Reviewer
—Publicity Agent
—Writer
—Foreign
    Correspondent
—Magazine Editor

Musical
—Musician
—Singer
—Band Leader
—Song Writer
—Music Critic
—Music Teacher
—Sound Producer

Social Service
  (interest in others'
  welfare)
—Nurse
—Boy or Girl
    Scout Leader
—Vocational
    Counselor

__Welfare Worker
—Minister
—Personnel Worker
—Social Worker
__Hospital Attendant
—Teacher
—Librarian
—Farm Advisor
—Interpreter

Clerical and (Numer-
  ical) Computational
—Bookkeeper
—Census Clerk
—Accountant
—File Clerk
—Bank Teller
—Sales Clerk
—Secretary
—Statistician
—Traffic Manager
—Comptometer
    Clerk
—Cost of Living
    Compiler
—Sales Manager
—Stenographer

5. Make a list of every vocation you have been interested in or thought of in recent years. Check them in the following manner, according to your preference or background: much (M), some (S), or none (N).

VOCATIONAL	LIKING				ABILITY IN				EXPERIENCE			CHOICE
	M	S	N		M	S	N		M	S	N	
Bank Clerk	X					X					X	2
Life Insurance Salesman		X				X				X		1
Production Manager		X					X			X		3

After you have finished you should be able to see a pattern in a group of related vocations in which you show interest, ability, and experience. This should help you decide better which vocational field to choose for your best interests.

INDEX